HOMECOMING

BASED ON THE BEST-SELLING VIDEOS

HOMECOMING

The Story of Southern Gospel Music
Through the Eyes of Its Best-Loved Performers

BILL GAITHER
with JERRY JENKINS

ZondervanPublishingHouse

Grand Rapids, Michigan

A Division of HarperCollinsPublishers

Homecoming
Copyright © 1997 by William J. Gaither and Jerry Jenkins

Requests for information should be addressed to:

ZondervanPublishingHouse
Grand Rapids, Michigan 49530

Library of Congress Cataloging-in-Publication Data

Gaither, Bill.
    Homecoming: the story of southern Gospel music through the eyes of its best-loved
performers / Bill Gaither with Jerry Jenkins.
       p.   cm.
    Includes index.
    ISBN: 0–310–21325-8 (hardcover)
     1. Gospel musicians—United States—Biography. 2. Gospel music—history and
criticism. I. Jenkins, Jerry B. II. Title.
ML385.G13   1997
782,24'4'092273—dc21   97–2707
  [b]   CIP

This edition printed on acid-free paper and meets the American National Standards Institute
Z39.48 standard.

Published in association with the literary agency of Alive Communications, 1465 Kelly
Johnson Blvd., Suite 320, Colorado Springs, CO 80920.

Interior design by Sherri L. Hoffman

Printed in the United States of America

97 98 99 00 01 02 03 04 /❖ DC/ 10 9 8 7 6 5 4 3 2 1

To those beloved musicians who have preceded us
in creativity,
in worship,
in sacred entertainment,
and in the unspeakable privilege
of being present with the Lord

Contents

Acknowledgments

With deep gratitude to Carolyn Hall, Shannon Kurtz, Rennie Rees,
tape transcriptionist Sherry Fischer,

James D. Walbert of Alabama, grandson of James D. Vaughan,

James R. Goff Jr., associate professor of history,

Appalachian State University, Boone, North Carolina,

and to all who generously contributed via interviews, photographs, and printed material.

Writer's Note

As a nonmusical lover of music, I had been a Bill Gaither devotee long before we first met in the early 1970s. Our paths crossed many times over the years as I wrote stories about him and Gloria for periodicals as disparate as *Moody Magazine* and *Reader's Digest.*

While working with him on his autobiography (*I Almost Missed the Sunset*) several years ago, I learned of the depth of his love for his roots in Southern gospel quartet music. He spoke longingly of the same names that had been musical heroes in my youth.

One family in our little Oakwood Bible Church in Kalamazoo, Michigan, also loved that style of music. In the 1950s, when Larry Bailey played his electric guitar and sang with his wife, Loretta, and Loretta's sister, Doris Price, we were treated to a rare privilege.

Larry always apologized to "any who don't appreciate this style of music," before his little trio sang "Mansion Over the Hilltop" or "Where Could I Go?" Maybe a few didn't appreciate it, but my brothers and I were not among them.

We enjoyed that same music at All Night Sings a couple of times a year at Kalamazoo's Central High School auditorium, where the Statesmen, the Blackwood Brothers, the Speer Family, and the LeFevres would appear. For days my brothers and I would pretend to get as low as J. D. Sumner or as high as Rosie Rozell.

Something is so rousing, so fun, and so emotional about this music that few can articulate it, even those who have devoted their lives to it. You can hear and understand every word, the harmonies are sweet and tight, the tenors high, the basses low, the piano fully employed. The lyrics are memorable and the melodies unforgettable, but something else sets this music apart.

Southern gospel, as with anything worthwhile and lasting, points to Jesus. When Bill Gaither got the idea of pulling his old friends and heroes back together, even he was unprepared for what happened.

You may be one of the millions who have enjoyed the videos. We hope you'll find a glimpse of some of your favorite people within these pages. After months of research, dozens of interviews, and a deluge of stories and pictures from everyone involved, we realized we had more than enough material for half a dozen such books.

So we have had to be painfully selective. You may have a favorite who is featured only in a photo here. We have tried to best represent Bill's exposure to Southern gospel, offer a brief history, and then let his friends tell their stories.

I have wept anew through nearly every viewing of the dozens of videos, because in the end, of course, there is but one Story. If you find Jesus reflected here, we will feel we have done justice to the world of Southern gospel music.

Jerry B. Jenkins
Zion, Illinois

The Authors

Bill Gaither, founder of the Gaither Music Company and originator of the Bill Gaither Trio and the Gaither Vocal Band, is one of the most celebrated Christian composers of the twentieth century. Several of his hundreds of songs have already become standards, including "Because He Lives," "He Touched Me," "There's Something About That Name," and "The King Is Coming."

The recipient of numerous Dove and Grammy awards, he was named Songwriter of the Year five times running and was inducted into the Gospel Music Association Hall of Fame in 1982. He and his wife, lyricist Gloria, live in Alexandria, Indiana, where Bill grew up. They have three grown children.

Among Jerry Jenkins' many titles are two *New York Times* best-sellers and six number-one Christian best-sellers. Formerly vice-president for publishing at the Moody Bible Institute of Chicago, he still serves Moody as writer-in-residence.

The current Gaither Vocal Band: Me, Guy Penrod, Mark Lowry, and Jonathon Pierce.

One

Homecoming

It's been said that big doors turn on small hinges. Often it's only from the perspective of years that we realize what monumental change can be wrought in our lives, based on what—at the time—seemed an insignificant decision.

That's how I feel about the Homecoming video series and the book you hold in your hands. In 1991 we had what we thought was a pretty good idea, and now, a little more than half a decade later, it has taken us for the ride of a lifetime.

The idea was simple. I was fifty-five years old and believed our time in music—Gloria's and mine—was pretty much past. We had raised three children and had seen the audience for our music begin to season with us.

We had enjoyed more than our share of ministry opportunities, honors, and success. Just as in the sports world, there's always someone younger in music who can do things in a better, fresher way. We were seeing that happen, and we were happy to do something a little different. We would keep publishing, keep finding and promoting new talent, and even keep performing—as long as we had an audience. But we were ready to move out of the spotlight and step aside for the new generation of Christian musicians.

A dream come true for Larry Gatlin, getting to sing with some of his heroes, each at one time a member of the Weatherford Quartet: Lily Weatherford, Glen Payne, and George Younce. Glen and George lead the Cathedrals.

On what I thought would be our last project, I wanted to do one song with my heroes. In 1991 the Gaither Vocal Band consisted of Mark Lowry, Jim Murray, Michael English, and me. On February 19 of that year we invited to the Master's Touch Studio in Nashville a host of legends to record with us one old Southern-style song, "Where Could I Go (But to the Lord)?" We chose that song, hoping we might place it on some country television. We booked the studio for the whole day, just for that one piece.

It was a logistical nightmare, locating and rounding up several singers whose work I had admired for decades. And if I thought *my* time was past, most of these friends were past typical retirement age. They were no longer household names. Had it not been for the phenomenon of the video network that sprang up

from this first little taping, few under age forty might know their names today.

It was a whole lot of fun, the Vocal Band singing with many of the treasures of legendary Southern gospel music. The Speer Family was there, along with George Younce and Glen Payne of the Cathedrals, James Blackwood, Hovie Lister, Jake Hess, J. D. Sumner and the Stamps, Howard and Vestal Goodman, Eva Mae LeFevre, Buck Rambo, Larry and Rudy Gatlin of the Gatlin Brothers, and many others.

We spent the morning working on that song, and I confess to a lump in the throat as we sang the beautiful old tune by James B. Coats.

The morning went well, and I felt we had gotten enough for a good one-song video. After lunch we gathered around the piano to take a picture, and fortunately

Eva Mae LeFevre of the LeFevres.

inisced about others, traded places at the piano, and sang a bunch of old favorite songs.

Where Could I Go?

Living below in this old sinful world,
Hardly a comfort can afford;
Striving alone to face temptations sore,
Where could I go but to the Lord?

Neighbors are kind, I love them every one,
We get along in sweet accord;
But when my soul needs manna from above,
Where could I go but to the Lord?

Life here is grand with friends I love so dear,
Comfort I get from God's own Word;
Yet when I face the chilling hand of death,
Where could I go but to the Lord?

Where could I go, O where could I go,
Seeking a refuge for my soul?
Needing a friend to help me in the end,
Where could I go but to the Lord?[1]

someone had the foresight to leave one video camera rolling and one microphone on. Because once the photograph was finished, Larry Gatlin said, "Eva Mae, play something."

Eva Mae, great matriarch of the LeFevres, began to play the piano as only she could. Soon the group began to sing. The next three hours seemed magic. We began to talk about who was there, who was not there, and who would love to be there. We prayed for some, rem-

We had no arrangements for anything except the song we had sung all morning. There was no sophisticated lighting, and at some points you can see people moving the microphone, closing the piano lid, and making room for someone who had spontaneously joined a song. We prompted some with lyrics and begged others to start a verse.

What a thrill it was to see young and old singing the great songs together, harmonizing, weeping, embracing. The Spirit of God was in that place. I was deeply moved, and I was grateful that there might be a second

Jim Murray, well-known tenor, formerly of the Imperials and more recently of the Gaither Vocal Band, now a soloist.

Ivan Parker and Willie Wynn, longtime first tenor of the Oak Ridge Boys, singing a song they made popular, "I Know."

Howard and Vestal Goodman.

Howard and Vestal Goodman.

or two of video from that afternoon of spontaneity that might find its way onto the "Where Could I Go?" video.

When the company that produced the single video said they had gotten what they wanted, I asked what they were going to do with the leftover raw footage. I knew there were two or three hours worth of some interesting music, though it had not been professionally staged.

They told me they were planning to discard it, so I asked for it. If nothing else, I wanted to relive that special afternoon myself. When I finally got around to taking the footage home and popping it into the VCR, I was stunned by how it communicated. I knew it wasn't of a quality I would be proud to broadcast or show off as the best we could do in the studio, but the sheer emotion and love that came through when those pioneers of Southern gospel worked together was a precious treasure.

I decided to produce a short video (less than an hour) called "The Gaither Vocal Band Homecoming Video Album" that would start with the "Where Could I Go?" session and include some of the good and usable moments of the impromptu afternoon. One of the highlights for me was when Jim Hill, now in his sixties, led the way on his own composition, "What a Day That Will Be."

What a Day That Will Be

There is coming a day when no heartaches shall come,
No more clouds in the sky, no more tears to dim the eye;
All is peace forevermore on that happy golden shore.
What a day, glorious day that will be!

There'll be no sorrow there, no more burdens to bear,
No more sickness, no pain, no more parting over there;
And forever I will be with the One who died for me.
What a day, glorious day that will be!

What a day that will be when my Jesus I shall see,
And I look upon His face—the One who saved me by His
grace;
When He takes me by the hand and leads me through
the promised land.
What a day, glorious day that will be![2]

Mark Lowry of the Gaither Vocal Band, clown prince of Southern gospel.

In 1954 Jim had founded a quartet called the Golden Keys, of which my brother Danny had been a member. Jim was one of the first to start making wide use of my music. People would ask him, "Where are you getting those songs?"

He'd say, "From Bill Gaither."

They'd say, "Who's Bill Gaither?"

I owe Jim a lot for that early confidence, but the whole church is indebted to him for his most revered song—one I wish I had written.

How we missed the great songwriter Dottie Rambo that day! Her husband Buck was there, but the composer of standards such as "We Shall Behold Him" and "If That Isn't Love" was suffering with back problems so severe that she couldn't travel. As far as Gloria and I are concerned, Dottie is what we call an original, and her writing reflects that. There are a lot of imitative writers out there, but Dottie copies no one. We respect her as one of the greatest living poets in Christendom today, and we honored her that day by singing one of her standards.

If That Isn't Love

He left the splendor of heaven,
Knowing His destiny
Was the lonely hill of Golgotha,
There to lay down His life for me.

Even in death He remembered
The thief hanging by His side,
He spoke with love and compassion,
Then He took him to paradise.

If that isn't love, the ocean is dry;
There's no stars in the sky, and the sparrow can't fly!
If that isn't love, then heaven's a myth,
There's no feeling like this, if that isn't love.[3]

HAVE YOU HAD A GETHSEMANE?

by

William J. Gaither

as sung and recorded by

The Golden Keys Quartet

of Portsmouth, Ohio

Sole Distributors –
Golden Key Distributors
4358 Gims Road
Portsmouth, Ohio

Here is the sheet music cover for one of my first compositions. From l: Pat Duncan, my brother Danny, Clarence Claxson, Harold Patrick, and Jim Hill (with his first quartet).

The Singing Rambos, 1968, (women seated l to r) Reba Rambo, Dottie Rambo, (top l) pianist Darius Spurgeon, (top r) Buck Rambo.

We sang a lot of great old songs that day, and several told touching stories too. Watching that raw footage, I was reminded of what makes some songs last and become standards, while hundreds written the same year seem to pass into oblivion. I'm convinced that the songs that reach the heart are foremost about Jesus Himself, but also those that have lifetime perspective seem to make the most sense. Songs that "stick to the wall," I like to say, have eternity in them.

Such songs are usually written by people who have been through deep water. Like C. Albert Tindley, they can say with credibility,

Take your burden to the cross and leave it there.
If you trust and never doubt, He will surely bring you out;
Take your burden to the cross and leave it there.[4]

They can write, with W. B. Stevens,

Farther along, we'll know all about it.
Farther along, we'll understand why.

Jim Hill, me, Joe Thrasher of the Thrasher Brothers, and Bill Shaw (20-year tenor with the Blackwood Brothers).

Cheer up my brother, live in the sunshine,
We'll understand it all by and by.[5]

That "by and by" could mean heaven, or it could mean that things that look bleak at age twenty-five will come into sharper focus when you're forty-five.

Those kinds of songs carry the big picture, the long view. That's what sets the good songs apart. It's not just that they're old. There are thousands of old songs we never hear anymore. These have survived because of the slice of eternity they contain.

Maybe someone is losing a child or a spouse. Maybe they're being abandoned. Can a lyric like Andraé Crouch's "Through It All" help a person going through that? I think so.

Through it all, through it all, I've learned to
trust in Jesus, I've learned to trust in God.
Through it all, through it all, I've learned to
depend upon His Word.[6]

The more I worked with the footage and tried to put it into the best format, the more I was moved. Larry Gatlin told how, as children, he and his brothers were exposed to the Blackwoods and the Statesmen and that the Gatlins have always considered those groups the impetus for their singing career.

James Blackwood told of the choir at Mom Speer's funeral, which had been made up of quartets and singing groups. "I couldn't sing," James told us that day. "I just cried and nodded."

Jake Hess sang his trademark "Prayer Is the Key to Heaven (But Faith Unlocks the Door)," and we could all sense the fervor and meaning of every quavery note as his long life and career and physical battles played into his rendering.

The younger people seemed in awe of the oldsters, and I realized that while there had been many multi-group concerts in the past, many of these people had never sung together. What a great choir it was, even if we weren't prepared to produce it the way I'd like to.

I added a few still shots of some of the old groups and tied it together with a bit of narration. I ended it with a poem from our dear, late friend Bob Benson, who had once said, "There has to be a song."

Well, there certainly was a song that day, and I like to think it made the Lord happy. I like to imagine Him nudging one of the angels while those sweet old-timers were harmonizing, and saying, "Listen to 'em sing. Isn't that beautiful?"

The LeFevres with little Troy Lumpkin (middle).

Bob Crews in his first organized group, the Sugar Hill Quartet, sometimes better known as the Midget Quartet, Scottsville, Kentucky in 1934. From l: Woodrow Gossage, Bob, Wilmer Glasgow, and Emmett Harlan.

There Has to Be a Song

There has to be a song—
There are too many dark nights,
Too many troublesome days,
Too many wearisome miles.
There has to be a song—
To make our burdens bearable,
To make our hopes believable,
To transform our successes into praise
To release the chains of past defeat.
Somewhere—down deep in a forgotten
corner of each man's heart—
There has to be a song.
Like a cool, clear drink of water,
Like the gentle warmth of the sunshine,
Like the tender love of a child,
There has to be a song.[7]

Several who reviewed the finished product agreed we had something special. We offered it to people we thought might enjoy a quasi-documentary about this kind of music and these people. We sensed more than the usual buzz of excitement and response for what we considered a modest video release. Then a producer for *The 700 Club* saw it and called me.

"I'd like to use this on the air and offer it for sale," he said.

"You've got to be kidding," I said. "That's not a network quality cut of stuff. It's got a home-movie feel to

Harmoneers Quartet (top l to r): Charles Key,
Happy Edwards, (middle) Low Note Hilton,
Bob Crews, (seated) Fred C. Maples.

Bob Crews—original lead singer of the Harmoneers on RCA Victor Records in the 1940s—
and Les Beasley of the Florida Boys.

it. One camera, one mike, not much thought given to the lighting and staging."

"I want to run it just as it is," he said.

He should have asked if we were prepared to keep up with the demand the airing would create. As soon as the video was shown, the 800-number lines were jammed at the Christian Broadcasting Network and we started producing tens of thousands of those tapes. Three weeks later they ran it again, and the response went through the roof again.

Every day our mail contained letters from people who had seen it and wanted to know if we had anything else like it. I wondered if it could be duplicated and began dreaming of the possibilities. What if we did it on purpose? Would it look contrived? Would it be as moving? I envisioned an even larger group with more legendary names, several cameras, lights, microphones, arrangements done in advance.

I knew I couldn't argue with something that had happened spontaneously, because God was in it. But I

Longtime quartet singer Bob Crews at ten months in a potato patch, and in Japan in the 1940s.

decided to set the stage again and see what would happen. This time we would be better prepared to record the results on a twenty-four-track audio machine, making use of the latest technology.

That fall of 1991, during the National Quartet Convention, I called all the people who were in the original video and added about that many more—including such names as Glenn Allred, Les Beasley, Sue Dodge, Paul and Ann Downing, Ed Enoch, Larry Ford, my wife Gloria, my brother Danny, Joy Gardner, Ed Hill, Kenny Hinson, Harold Lane, Mylon LeFevre, Rex Nelon, Ed O'Neal,

Russ Taff, Earl and Lily Weatherford, and several others. Best of all, we were able to get Dottie Rambo this time.

A few of those from the original video pulled me aside and warned me, "Bill, you'll never capture what you captured on the first one, because we didn't know the cameras were on."

I carefully considered that advice, but I wanted to try it anyway. Maybe it wouldn't be the same. Who knew? Maybe, because of our preparation, it would be better. No, this wasn't something that could be manufactured. Anyone could produce nice cuts of music

Bob Crews today

when everyone involved gets a sense of what this is all about. Anyone in that studio has a healthy ego after having been on stage for decades. Even with the best motives, there's a natural struggle with the flesh.

But when ministry starts to happen, when emotions come to the surface, when people start realizing, "It's not about me; it's about Him," something changes. That's when we start to get footage that moves people to tears, moves them to change, moves them closer to God.

We called the second video "Reunion—A Gospel Homecoming Celebration" and again recorded in a Nashville studio, using the old Ryman Auditorium for cut-in interviews with several of the principals. The Ryman was, of course, the original Grand Ole Opry hall.

That place has a special place in my heart, because it was there in 1949 in a seat I can still point out, that I enjoyed my first live All-Night Singing. A man named Wally Fowler promoted these events, and I had heard of them on the radio and seen them advertised in the songbooks of various quartets marketed throughout the country.

I was in the eighth grade when my parents drove me from our home in Indiana to the Ryman Auditorium. I was nearly delirious with anticipation, insisting that we get there a couple of hours early so I could see how they put the whole thing together. I badgered my dad until he agreed to take me early, but he said, "For crying out loud, Bill, it's an all-night sing. If you go early I'm going to make you stay till it's over."

By about two-thirty the next morning, Dad probably wished he'd never made that threat. Only a few hundred faithfuls remained in the Ryman by then, but I was

with talent like that. My dream was that because of the nostalgia, the names involved, the songs we would include, and the atmosphere we would try to engender, something special would happen again.

I've found as we've done more and more of these that there comes a point, somewhere in the middle of the first day of taping (we now tape three straight days), one of them, hooked forever on an exciting, fun, dynamic form of entertainment and praise that would eventually lead me to Christ. All I ever wanted to do from that moment on was to become a pianist and vocalist for a Southern gospel quartet.

It was the thrill of a lifetime to return to the Ryman more than forty years later and use it as a backdrop for our second video, "Reunion—A Gospel Homecoming Celebration."

All the videos have had their highlights and super emotional moments, but I didn't realize until we were deep into the taping of this one that it would prove the most personally moving for Gloria and me. Bringing together all these old friends and forerunners made us as nostalgic as we had ever been, and by the end of the recording we would trade love songs and monologues that made "Reunion" the most intimate of them all.

Hamming it up with my friend George Younce of the Cathedrals on the floor of the National Quartet Convention in Louisville, 1996.

Two
Reunion

＊＊＊＊＊

Southern gospel has never been at a loss for great pianists. I couldn't begin to list the greats, some of whom still play today. It's fun to hear the women from some of the old groups, people like Eva Mae LeFevre and Rosa Nell (Speer) Powell. They have every bit of the style and showmanship of their male counterparts, seeming to use every key on every song.

Rosa Nell began at the piano in that second video, "Reunion—A Gospel Home-coming Celebration," and we all marveled at her still prodigious keyboard gift. She'd go fast and fancy, then slow and sweet, and you just had to move. Soon we put together a makeshift quartet representing four great groups: Ben Speer from the Speer Family, Vestal Goodman of the Happy Goodman Family, James Blackwood of the Blackwood Brothers, and George Younce of the Cathedrals. They sang "I'm Living in Canaan Now," and then five of the greatest bass singers in history began to gather.

What a group they made! George Younce was joined by Paul Downing of the Downings—who would die of a heart attack a few weeks later, Brock Speer (Speer Family), Rex Nelon (the Nelons), and J. D. Sumner (the Stamps Quartet). Those

rolling basses made an interesting sound, trying to sing parts and stay out of each others' ways on "Give the World a Smile Each Day."

What history that song carries! It had been the radio theme song of one of the earliest versions of the Stamps Quartet in the 1930s. The highlight of the five-bass version in the video was Wally Varner at the piano. For more than fifty years in the business, Wally has been considered one of the best and flashiest on the bench.

He was all over that keyboard, those still-nimble fingers flying, leaving us shaking our heads.

Some moments have to be experienced in person, but anyone who has seen James Blackwood's brief testimony after the group sang "Sheltered in the Arms of God" can sense the weight of the emotion that poured down on that place. James had had a stroke since the last time he was with us and tearfully thanked everyone for their concern and prayers. Someone asked him to take the lead on the second verse of that great Dottie Rambo and Jimmie Davis song.

James had said he felt only about seventy-five percent recovered, and while there may have been a bit of a labored beginning from the man already in his seventies, the legendary lead singer quickly warmed to the job, and again, the truth of the lyric made the moment all that more poignant.

Sheltered in the Arms of God

I feel the touch of hands so kind and tender,
They're leading me in the paths that I must trod;
I have no fear when Jesus walks beside me,
For I'm sheltered in the arms of God.

Soon I shall hear the call from heaven's portals,
"Come home, my child, it's the last mile you must
* trod";*
I'll fall asleep and wake in God's new Heaven,
Sheltered safe within the arms of God.

So let the storms rage high, the dark clouds rise,
They won't worry me, for I'm sheltered safe within the
* arms of God.*
He walks with me and naught of earth can harm me,
Sheltered safe within the arms of God.[1]

Later my good friends Glen Payne and George Younce of the Cathedrals sang with Earl and Lily Weatherford, just like in the old days. They sang, "I Will Be There Soon," none of us realizing that the song

Eva Mae LeFevre at her birthplace in McCall, South Carolina.

*Me with Marion Snider, original pianist
for the Stamps Quartet
(with whom he began in 1936).*

*One of the favorites in the Homecoming tapes,
Lily Weatherford, probably one of the greatest
female voices of all time in our industry.*

The Hinsons (from l): Ronny Hinson, Larry Hinson, Chris Freeman, Kenny Hinson (deceased).

would become literally true for Earl before we would meet again.

Another special moment in that video was Sue Dodge singing a great Dad Speer song, "I Never Shall Forget That Day," with Harold Lane and Faye and Brock Speer. They kept getting louder and faster, and finally Sue took the lead. She's one of those rare singers who hits every note right in the middle of the pitch, and everybody loved it so much they kept encouraging her to keep going. And she did. (Anyone who can carry a tune can find the pitch, but musicologists tell us that there are at least three gradations in every note. You can be north or south of the exact pitch and still get by—I'm one of those who slides south more often than north—but those who can hit it right in the middle are rare. They can carry an entire group of singers.)

It was hard to top the emotion in the studio as the time slowly passed and the end of the session neared. With his mother at the piano, Mylon LeFevre, now in his fifties, sang a song he had written as a seventeen-year-old, "Without Him." Mylon had been the very definition of a prodigal son for many years, having left his family and seemingly his faith, as he tasted what the world had to offer.

The LeFevres (from l): Mylon, Pierce, Jimmy Jones, Alphus, Rex Nelon, (seated) Eva Mae, and Urias.

But finally God wooed back the one who had so early in his life beautifully expressed what he could only fully understand now in maturity.

Without Him

Without Him I could do nothing,
Without Him I'd surely fail;
Without Him I would be drifting,
Like a ship without a sail.

Without Him I could be dying,
Without Him I'd be enslaved;
Without Him life would be hopeless,
But with Jesus, thank God, I'm saved.

Jesus, O Jesus,
Do you know Him today?
You can't turn Him away,
O Jesus, O Jesus,
Without him how lost I would be.[2]

Henry Slaughter, who with his wife, Hazel, traveled with us for ten years. We have no better friends.

Hazel Slaughter.

Stuart Hamblen, dramatic convert through the 1949 Billy Graham Crusade and writer of many popular songs, including "This Ole House."

It had been an incredible several hours in the studio, and I knew we had enough to make a good video. But I wanted to sing Gloria a love song. One of my favorites, which means more to me today than ever, was written by one of my songwriter-heroes, Stuart Hamblen. After turning to Christ at a Billy Graham crusade in Los Angeles in 1949, the same year I had attended my first all-night singing in Nashville, he wrote many famous songs, including "It Is No Secret (What God Can Do)," "Until Then," and "This Ole House."

I chose one of his later tunes to sing to Gloria, and it was all I could do to maintain my composure as I stood before her and sang, surrounded by so many of our treasured friends.

Tho' Autumn's Coming On

*Thru changing seasons we've shared life's little day,
Still in love though autumn's coming on;
It seems unreal, our souvenirs still look so new,
We reminisce and must confess that this is true.
We sang lullabies to babies' cries of springtime,
O how the time seemed to fly;
We had scarcely put the crib away when like magic,
We looked up the aisle and beheld a lovely bride.
We waved goodbye as one by one they joined life's
 parade,
When at a bugle call, he stood proud and tall, there
 went our baby;
Those seasons change, hand in hand we travel on,
Still in love though autumn's coming on.[3]*

Gloria had prepared a reading for me too, but I shouldn't have scheduled myself to play piano under her narration. I didn't have a hand free as the tears cascaded. Here's what she read to me that day:

I first heard about you from a college friend who loved gospel quartets and had heard you and your brother and sister sing at an all-night singing in Detroit.

When she found out I was going to fill in for a teacher at the high school where you taught, she couldn't wait for me to meet you and then for me to get her a date with your brother.

I never did get her a date with your brother, but I did fall in love with you. Little did I know that this English teacher with the crew cut and weird sense of humor, who talked about politics and literature, had another love. But I was soon to find out.

After we had dated long enough to know that this was more than just another social relationship, you took me to your parents' farm where you lived and played me a couple of songs by a group called the Speer Family.

When the songs were through you asked what I thought. I said I liked the songs, and you said you wrote

Roy and Amy Pauley are singers from Florida, and Roy is also a columnist for the Singing News.

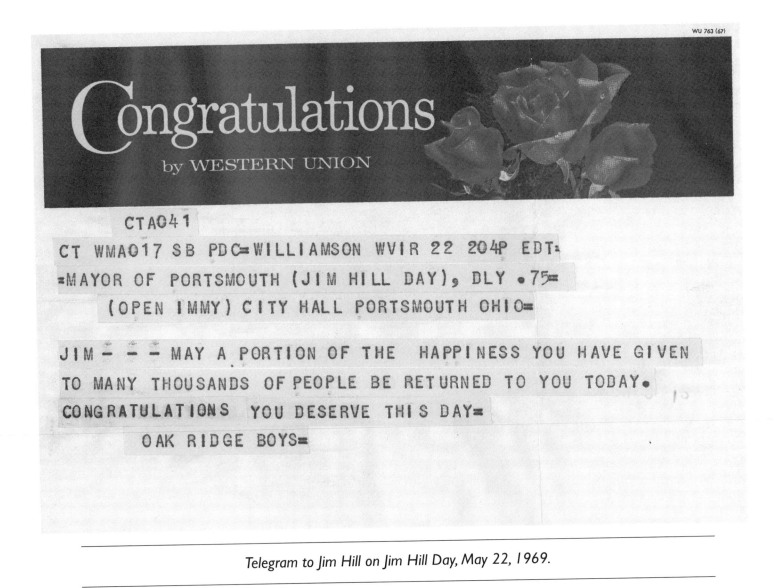

Congratulations
by WESTERN UNION

CTA041

CT WMA017 SB PDC=WILLIAMSON WVIR 22 204P EDT=
=MAYOR OF PORTSMOUTH (JIM HILL DAY), DLY .75=
(OPEN IMMY) CITY HALL PORTSMOUTH OHIO=

JIM = = = MAY A PORTION OF THE HAPPINESS YOU HAVE GIVEN
TO MANY THOUSANDS OF PEOPLE BE RETURNED TO YOU TODAY.
CONGRATULATIONS YOU DESERVE THIS DAY=
    OAK RIDGE BOYS=

Telegram to Jim Hill on Jim Hill Day, May 22, 1969.

them. The songs were "I've Been to Calvary" and "The Joy of Serving the Lord."

Then you played me recordings by the Statesmen, the Blackwoods, and finally Jim Hill singing "Lovest Thou Me?" and "The Old Fashioned Meeting." I asked if you wrote those songs, and you said you did. I've often wondered what might have become of us had I not been impressed by those songs.

After I passed my "initiation" we would often end our Saturday night dates driving through the Indiana countryside listening through the come-and-go reception to see if J. Bazzel Mull would play any of your songs on his gospel radio show.

Since Southern gospel music was not a part of my heritage, I had a lot to learn. You were a walking encyclopedia of strange names, song titles, group personnel, and all-night

Stan Whitmire, a young pianist, gets tips from one of the great keyboard artists in our field, Rosie (Rosa Nell Speer) Powell.

singing tour schedules. You knew who played piano for the Rangers in 1952, what bass singer sang when for the Foggy River Boys, and which tenors had ever sung with the Homeland Harmony Boys. The names you rattled off I was certain you made up, but I was soon to learn that there really was someone named J. Bazzel Mull and Denver Crumpler.

Though we began to write songs together and soon to tell with one family combination or another the story of what God was doing in our own lives, still you couldn't resist stopping by a gospel sing somewhere now and then to hear the Weatherfords or Wendy Bagwell and the Sunlighters, the Statesmen, or the Speer Family, and of course the Blackwood Brothers and the Happy Goodman Family.

You even did some promoting in our area and made me go with you to tack up posters and flyers all over central Indiana, announcing a new group called the Imperials with Jake Hess and Henry Slaughter.

I'll never forget the night our son was to be born. I was in the first stages of labor, but I had to hold off till you got home from an all-night sing in Indianapolis, where you had gone to hear just a few groups, you said, and deliver some sheet music. That night, I'll have to admit, was not the night I loved gospel music the best.

Over the years, these names I thought you made up first became real people to me, then precious friends. Vestal and Howard Goodman, Brock and Faye Speer, Hovie and Jake, Buck and Dottie Rambo, Henry Slaughter and Hazel, and so many more have become dear to us both.

I remember holding our little Suzanne by the seat of the pants while her little legs danced up and down on the back of our couch to "I Wouldn't Take Nothin' For My Journey Now." And I couldn't count the summer nights when we've piled all three of our kids, wrapped in blankets in the old red convertible, and driven out under the starry Indiana sky singing in family harmony, "Jesus Is Coming Soon," while the crickets and cicadas sang their counterparts.

Now our kids are writing songs of their own, singing harmonies with their kids, and making demos better than we ever learned to make. Once again, it's just you and me, Babe. And more and more I notice you getting out the old records that started you on this journey, or sitting down after supper to play again a few measures of some song you used to pretend to broadcast out the window of that old farmhouse in Scotts Addition when you came home from Cunningham School.

For these are the songs that got your attention, captured your imagination, and showed you the way to Jesus. And the harmonies you loved became the seed of your dreams, dreams we have together realized more than you, even you, could have ever imagined.[4]

The 1968 Bill Gaither Trio: (back) my brother, Danny, my wife, Gloria, and me.

Old Friends

Old friends, after all of these years,
Just old friends, through the laughter and years,
Old friends, what a find! What a priceless treasure!
Old friends, like a rare piece of gold,
Old friends make it great to grow old;
Till then, through it all I will hold to old friends.

God must have known that some days on our own,
We would lose our will to go on;
That's why He sent friends like you along.

Old friends, yes you've always been there,
My old friends, we've had more than our share,
Old friends, I'm a rich millionaire in old friends.

A phone call, a letter, a pat on the back,
Or a "Hey, I just dropped in to say,"
A hand when we're down, a loan when we just couldn't pay;
A song or a story, a rose from the florist,
A little note that you just happened to send out of the blue
Just to tell us that you're still our friend.[1]

Doris Akers, beloved songwriter of "Sweet, Sweet Spirit," "I Cannot Fail the Lord," and many others.

Three
Old Friends

I want to tell you about the phenomenon of the third video, "Old Friends," before getting into a little personal history of how I came to love this music and then a brief history of the musical style itself.

We thought it would be fun to kick this whole idea into high gear and invite a hundred or so of the best people and groups from the past and present to our own Pinebrook Studios in Alexandria, Indiana.

That way we could plan ahead, have total control, and serve as hosts for all those guests. We put them up in nearby hotels, fed them, offered makeup help, and planned the days of taping in advance—including an order of songs that made sense, some prearranging, staging, lighting, and all the rest. We had been thrilled with the success of the first two videos, but our feeling was, "If you liked those, you're going to love this." The plan was to give the singers, the studio, and the tape every advantage to succeed at every level.

There would still be spontaneity, and we would certainly allow God to move in His own way and at His own time. We simply wanted the right people in the right place at the right time. We even wrote a new piece for the occasion.

Doris Akers.

Gloria opened the video with this brief thought: "Perhaps the greatest treasure on earth and one of the only things that will survive this life is human relationships: old friends. We are indeed rich if we have friends. Friends who have loved us through the problems and heartaches of life. Deep, true, joyful friendships. Life is too short and eternity too long to live without old friends."

That day we added to our usual list with a few more contemporary artists and a whole lot of people from some of the longest-running groups of all. Naomi Sego—who along with her brothers James and W. R. made up a popular group in the '50s and '60s, the Sego Brothers and Naomi—was there with her new group.

I love all the singers, of course, but a huge thrill for me is when the old songwriters join us too. That day we had Doris Akers with us. Most famous for her standard, "Sweet, Sweet Spirit," she wrote more than 500 gospel songs after learning to play the piano by ear at age six.

I wanted to accompany Doris on the piano while she sang her own, "Sweet Jesus," but apparently I wasn't capturing the rhythm the way she liked it. The dynamic, engaging, little old lady just booted me off the bench and took over playing herself, much to the delight of the rest of the singers!

We couldn't know that Doris would fall victim to spinal cancer and would not be with us long after that. That day we simply enjoyed her, as the rest of us went from performers to backup choir and finally to just cheering audience as she regaled us.

Sweet Jesus

There's a Name that's dear to me, lifted me from misery,
Took me out of sin and shame, how I love His blessed Name;
It gets sweeter every day, serving Jesus really pays,
Oh, how I love this man of Galilee.

If the Lord you've never known, you should hasten to His throne,
Such a blessing you'll receive, if in Him you will believe,

The Florida Boys of 1960 (from l): Cory Cook, Les Beasley, Derrell Stewart, Glenn Allred, Billy Todd.

Life will be so sweet to you, you'll call Him,
    Sweet Jesus, too,
Oh, how I love this man of Galilee.

Sweet Jesus, fellowship divine,
Sweet Jesus, I'm His and He is mine,
Sweet Jesus, a precious Friend indeed,
Sweet Jesus, whenever I'm in need;
Fellowship divine, I'm His and He is mine,
A precious Friend indeed, whenever I'm in need,
Oh, how I love this man of Galilee.[2]

The Florida Boys were there, and three of them—Les Beasley, Glenn Allred, and Derrell Stewart—had been together for about forty years. Their bass, Buddy Liles, joined the group in 1972. Their newest member, Greg Cook, addressed us all early in the taping:

When Les told me we were coming to do this, my first question was, "Why am I going to be there?" I feel so unworthy just sitting in this room, looking at all of you who have paved the way. [The Florida Boys] will never know

Jim Hill and Doug Oldham, beloved gospel singers who helped introduce many of my earliest compositions.

what they did for me, because I know how green I am, and I know I'm not the best they could have had. But thank God He gave me the opportunity to sing the music that I love … I give all the glory and all the praise to the only star in gospel music, and that's the Lord Jesus Christ.

It was a special thrill for me to have Doug Oldham join us. He has been identified by many as the best interpreter of my type of song. We go back a long way, and in fact it was his father who suggested, because of the great change God had brought into Doug's life and marriage, that I write a song called "He Touched Me." Doug was the first to sing it, and he and I are probably both more identified with that song than anything else either of us has ever done.

He Touched Me

Shackled by a heavy burden,
'Neath a load of guilt and shame,
Then the hand of Jesus touched me,
And now I am no longer the same.

Since I met this blessed Savior,
Since He cleansed and made me whole,
I will never cease to praise Him;
I'll shout it while eternity rolls:

He touched me, oh, He touched me.
And, oh, the joy that floods my soul.
Something happened and now I know,
He touched me and made me whole.[3]

The Happy Goodman Family: Howard and his two brothers, Rusty and Sam, and his sisters, 1948. This was before Vestal came into Howard's life and into the singing ministry.

Doug has a profound effect on his audience, even when it is made up of his peers, contemporary and historic. Doug stepped to the microphone during the "Old Friends" video taping to sing "Thanks to Calvary," and by the time he was finished, he had sung three of my songs.

Thanks to Calvary

Today I went back to the place where I used to go,
Today I saw the same old crowd I knew before;
When they asked me what had happened I tried
*   to tell them,*
"Thanks to Calvary I don't live here anymore."

And then we went back to the house where we used to live,
My little girl ran and hid behind the door;
I said, "Honey, never fear, you've got a new daddy,
Thanks to Calvary I don't live here anymore."

Thanks to Calvary I am not the man I used to be,
Thanks to Calvary things are different than before;
While the tears ran down my face, I tried to tell her,
"Thanks to Calvary I don't live here anymore."[4]

Doug often weeps when he sings, and I weep when I hear him. That day it seemed everyone in the room took the lyrics to heart and applied them personally to their own histories.

After also singing "I'm Free," we couldn't let Doug go without his always rousing rendition of "The King Is Coming."

The King Is Coming

The marketplace is empty,
No more traffic in the streets,
All the builders' tools are silent,
No more time to harvest wheat;
Busy housewives cease their labors,
In the courtroom no debate,
Work on earth is all suspended
As the King comes through the gate.

Happy faces line the hallways
Those whose lives have been redeemed,
Broken homes that He has mended,
Those from prison He has freed;
Little children and the aged
Hand in hand stand all aglow,
Who were crippled, broken, ruined,
Clad in garments white as snow.

I can hear the chariots rumble,
I can see the marching throng,
The flurry of God's trumpets
Spells the end of sin and wrong;
Regal robes are now unfolding,
Heaven's grandstands all in place,
Heaven's choir is now assembled,
Start to sing "Amazing Grace!"

O the King is coming, the King is coming!
I just heard the trumpets sounding, and now
*   His face I see;*
O the King is coming, the King is coming!
Praise God, He's coming for me![5]

One of the senior statesmen of the Southern gospel field, Rex Nelon, is also an outstanding publisher. He owns such titles as "O What A Savior," "The Night Before Easter," and Vep Ellis's "The Love of God."

Another special moment came that day when Howard and Vestal Goodman were joined by Johnny Cook and George Younce, with Terry McMillan on harmonica, and they sang a creation by Howard's late brother Rusty. His "I Wouldn't Take Nothin' For My Journey Now" had been inspired by a comment Rusty overheard from a preacher. It's a robust, fun song and real challenge to the tongue of any singer, even the ven-

erable Vestal, who moves a hundred miles an hour to get every syllable to match the pace of the music. Since he wrote it in the 1960s, this tune has become a standard and a favorite of lovers of Southern gospel.

The Happy Goodman Family, initially made up of Howard Goodman and his huge family of brothers and sisters, really exploded on to the scene of gospel music in the 1960s when the group was refined to include Howard, his wife Vestal, and Howard's brothers Sam and Charles (Rusty).

They had a unique sound, with Vestal one of those loud, country-style lead singers who could hit the pitch dead in the middle (like Glen Payne of the Cathedrals, Sue Dodge, James Blackwood in his prime, and only a few others) and still can after decades in the ministry. Rusty was a perfectionist who was always trying to make the group better musically. He was a gifted writer and a wonderful man, and we all missed him and Sam that day. They had died within eleven months of each other a few years before.

I Wouldn't Take Nothin' for My Journey Now

There's nothin' in the world that'll ever take the
place of God's love.
Silver and gold could never buy His love from above;
When my soul needs healin' and I begin to feelin' His
power,
I can say, "Thank the Lord, I wouldn't take nothin'
for my journey now."

I started out travelin' for the Lord many years ago.
I've had a lotta heartaches, met a lotta grief and woe;
And when I would stumble, then I would humble down,
And there I would say, "I wouldn't take nothin' for my
journey now."

Well, I wouldn't take nothin' for my journey now,
I've gotta make it up to heaven somehow;
Tho' the devil tempts me and tries to turn me around;
He's offered everything that's got a name:
All the wealth I want and worldly fame;
If I could, still I wouldn't take nothin' for my journey now.[6]

The world is hurting from a shortage of lovers—people who feel what others feel, people of compassion. There is too much pain and too little joy. Too many wounds and not enough balm. Too much alienation and not enough belonging. Too much confusion and not enough direction. Too much loneliness and not enough compassion. Too much betrayal and not enough faithfulness. Too many tears in the night and not enough arms to enfold. The world is hurting from a shortage of lovers.

The world is oblivious, for there are too few visionaries. Too blind to subtleties and too impressed by carnivals. Too numb to gentleness and too overwhelmed by power. Too deaf to music and too stimulated by noise. Too dull to recognize the permanent—too focused on the transient. Too tuned out to the prophets, too attuned to the hucksters. The world is oblivious for there are too few visionaries.

The world is losing heart, for there are too few dreamers. Too much cynicism and not enough faith. Too much hype and not enough hope. Too much savvy and not enough wisdom. Too much money and not enough treasure. Too much form and not enough substance. Too

For the "Old Friends" video, we showed a clip of a tribute to Rusty that had been taped in September of 1990, when his health was failing. Gloria had written a personal tribute to him for that occasion, and we re-ran it on the video. It went like this:

Gloria, my poet laureate, with Eva Mae LeFevre, matriarch of the LeFevre family.

Another great songwriter, Audrey Mieir, on the cover of one of her piano books. She wrote "His Name Is Wonderful," among many others.

Not long before her death, Audrey posed with husband Charles, whom she always called the wind beneath her wings.

many takers and not enough givers. Too many dissenters and not enough inspirers. The world is losing heart, for there are too few dreamers.

Ira Stanphill, along with Stuart Hamblen, Albert Brumley, Doris Akers, and Mosie Lister, is in a category set apart from most songwriters. They wrote many songs that will live and stick in the church in the coming century. They're some of the best.

Into such a world, God sends his poets/prophets/troubadours who see what we have missed, who warn us lest we self-destruct, and who fill the songless night with music. They surround our alienation with love's embrace; they burn through the fog of our oblivion with the piercing lights of truth, and they sing the dream back into our hearts. They tune our ears to the laughter of children; they raise our sights to lofty aspirations; they help us discriminate between the tinsel and the true. Poets are the contemplatives in the heart of the world. Without them we would settle into the fatal monotony of our comfort zones and accept the clouded vision of cataracted perception.

Rusty Goodman is such a poet/troubadour. He sees and helps us see what we might have missed. He notices a grin in an elevator and puts value in a handshake. He reminds the breaking heart that there is the promise of the new dawn and points out to us battle-weary soldiers that we're almost home. When we've lost someone we love, Rusty, you've told us of a greater love we can never lose, a love of our very own. When we have been tempted to put too much store in what we have or what we know, you've reminded us that we have really known nothing 'til we know the love of God. When we've focused on our failures, you pointed us to the Potter who doesn't patch up a broken vessel but puts it back on the wheel and remolds it into something brand new. When we struggle for some sense of worth, when we feel insignificant, you sing to us of a God who cared about robins that fall, lilies of the field, wind-ravaged trees, and frightened sailors in a storm, and assure us that He will speak peace to the storms in us because He loves us infinitely more. We've found ourselves more than once—because of you—singing at the top of our lungs: "If I could, still I wouldn't take nothin' for my journey now." Thank you for that! And even though we know

Lily Weatherford at age 16, with (from l) Roy Jones, Bob Gillis, and husband Earl.

that for a long time now, you've had leavin' on your mind, we're asking you to stay, because we need—and this old world needs—what you are to us: a lover, a visionary, a dreamer, a poet. We need you here to walk with us and sing your pilgrim's song.[7]

There were a host of precious moments that day, and then we finished with the incomparable Jake Hess singing Mosie Lister's wonderful "Then I Met the Master." What a thrill it was to have Mosie in the studio with

us that day! With Doris Akers, Audrey Mieir, Ira Stanphill, and Stuart Hamblen, Mosie is one of my all-time songwriter heroes. For more than fifty years, he has been a leader in gospel music with hundreds of songs to his credit. "Goodby, World, Goodby," "Happy Rhythm," and "How Long Has It Been" are three of his standards. But "Then I Met the Master" ranks right up there with them, and, of course, no one interprets a song or puts as much of himself into it as dear Jake.

In his own book *Good Ol' Gospel—35 All-Time Favorite Songs by Mosie Lister*, Mosie tells of the writing of this classic:

This song has been such a comfort to so many people, and at the same time kind of a challenge. At first I didn't realize it was going to be that. I wrote it because I wanted to describe what happened to Jesus' disciples. They were living one kind of life before they met Him. Then after they met Him and knew Him, they lived a completely different kind of life. That's what I wanted to say.

Once I got into writing the song, I realized it was getting emotional (and a lot of my songs are emotional; that's the way I am. I try to say what is true and right, and I try to say

it in an original way, using some phrases that haven't been used a lot). So I began by comparing my former state with a blind man who cannot see, and with a baby who is helpless; then saying that all things were different after I met Him, because after I met Him, I realized that I completely belonged to Him.

I got word that a teenage girl in Bradenton, Florida, was singing this song as she lay dying. When I heard that, I wept. I don't know which phrase she sang last, but I was glad that song was a comfort to her.

The song has also been instrumental in causing some to commit their lives to the Lord and causing some to answer the call to preach. It's been used in many marvelous ways. God has taken it and done far more than I ever thought could happen.[8]

Then I Met the Master

Like a babe when it cries for its mother,
Like a child I was helpless alone;
Then I met the Master, now I am one of His own.

Like a blind man who walks in the darkness,
I was lost and I searched for the Light;
Then I met the Master, now I walk no more
in the night.

For all things were changed when He found me,
A new day broke through all around me;
For I met the Master, now I am one of His own.
I met the Master, now I am one of His own.[9]

Kirk Talley, an outstanding soloist
and songwriter, now on his own.

Having taped that video in my hometown exceeded all the expectations I had carried since I was a young boy with a dream to spend my life in gospel music. Most of the musical heroes of my youth,

Bob Cain, a converted night club musician from Birmingham, Alabama, now a gospel soloist.

performers from many walks of life, from many different parts of the country.

Some had just experienced great victories, some had just experienced deep sorrow, some just wanted to come and drink it all in, and some just didn't want to miss all the fun. That's just like any group that gathers to enjoy each other's company and remember the One who brings us together in a bond that time and distance cannot erase.

along with many of the friends with whom we have shared the stage over our careers, and some of the brightest, new talent serving the Lord around this country, had gathered in our town to spend the day together just praising the Lord.

There were more Dove Awards, Grammy Awards, gold records, and Silver Eagle bus miles represented in that room than at any time and place I could ever remember. Many of those gracious artists were legends to those of us who love gospel music. There were

Larry Ford of Fort Myers, Florida, formerly of the Dixie Echoes and the Downings, is one of the great lyric tenors of our time.

The Kevin Spencer Family (from l): Kevin Spencer, Tammy Spencer, and Scott Bircher. Kevin created the popular "Homecoming Audition" trivia game.

The singing that day still rings in my ears. It was a day of great music, the joy of praising God, and the close fellowship of old friends. And you know, old friends never leave a room empty.

That studio is empty now, except for a stack of chairs, coils of different colored cords, and a dusty pile of paper scraps, cups, and flower petals. The risers have been stored, the plants returned to the florist, and the light trusses and television equipment loaded onto trucks.

Yes, the room is almost empty now, but it isn't silent. Echoes of a beautiful memory fill every corner. As our steps click across the parquet floor we seem to hear blendings of great Mosie Lister and Ira Stanphill songs being tossed back and forth between those who

have lived out the truth of the words learned long ago: the break in Jake's voice trying to cram a lifetime of certainty into one verse of "Then I Met the Master," Ira's sharing the story of painful days that "washed his eyes with tears," and Eva Mae LeFevre singing with sweet assurance "I've Got a Mansion Just Over the Hilltop."

There is a spirit in that room. Everywhere I turn I feel the spirit remaining like the sweet fragrance of expensive perfume after a dancer has whirled from the ballroom floor. There is the spirit of Kelly Nelon Thompson hugging her daddy, Rex Nelon, and Doris Akers shoving me off the piano bench when I couldn't get the rhythm right.

There is the sweet fragrance of two young men with shaky knees—one paying tribute to Gloria for

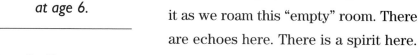

Lillie Knauls then...

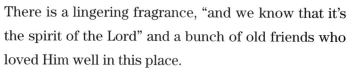

Lillie, already a hat-wearer at age 6.

Lillie today.

having taken him on a nature hike when he was a six-year-old and the other thanking his veteran quartet manager who gave him the chance to spend his life singing out his love for Jesus.

Another old song we used to sing says, "I can feel the brush of angel wings." Maybe that explains the stir in the air in this big vacant room. There was a lot of talk about heaven from people who had recently become most intimate with its hope. Lily Fern Weatherford

filled this room with the confidence that she would meet her beloved Earl "in the morning," and Vestal confirmed some specific things heaven means to her.

Kirk Talley, with tears streaming down his face, sang what all our hearts knew: "He is here; we can touch Him, and we'll never be the same."

You are right, Kirk. Today we know it as we roam this "empty" room. There are echoes here. There is a spirit here. There is a lingering fragrance, "and we know that it's the spirit of the Lord" and a bunch of old friends who loved Him well in this place.

The Fairfield Four (clockwise from top l): Robert Hamlett, Wilson Waters, Joe Rice, James Hill, and Isaac Freeman.

The 1954 Harvesters Quartet (from l): Bill Hefner, Buddy Parker, Don Norman, Bob Thacker, Jack Clark.

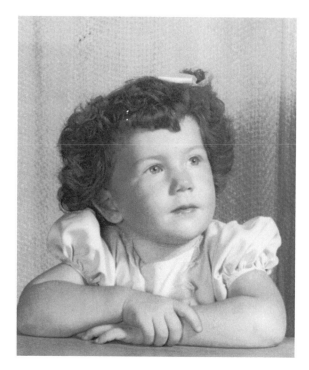

Cynthia Clawson, a major artist in her own right, now having success in the Southern gospel field. She used to travel with us.

Cynthia Clawson—whom we were proud to introduce to Southern gospel audiences— at ages 2 and 16.

LaBreeska and Joel Hemphill, popular songwriters and performers.

LaBreeska and Joel Hemphill in 1959. They had a group called the Hemphills and have written such tunes as "He's Still Working On Me," "Pity the Man," "When Jesus Says It's Enough," "Master of the Wind," and many others.

Candy Hemphill at 13 with her mother, LaBreeska, in 1974. Candy is a cut above as a soloist in our field.

Candy Hemphill Christmas with her own daughter, Jasmine, in 1989.

Jeff and Sheri Easter (middle)
with Greg Ritchie (l) and Steve Easter.

Jeff Easter with former Gaither Trio lead singer,
Gary McSpadden and Jeff's daughter, Morgan.

Tanya Goodman Sykes, daughter of the late Rusty Goodman, and Sheri Easter of Jeff and Sheri Easter. Sheri was Female Vocalist of the Year in the Singing Fan Awards for 1996.

Buddy Greene weaving his harmonica magic at the Texas Homecoming.

Give The World A Smile

Otis Deaton

M. L. Yandell

An example of shaped notes music.

1. Are you giv - ing to the world a smile, sun - ny smile, Help - ing
2. You may be a shin - ing light to - day, yes, to - day, Point - ing
3. Just a bright and sun - ny smile will win, it will win, Man - y

less - en some - one's drear - y mile, drear - y mile? Do you
souls to Heav - en's glo - ry - way, glo - ry - way, If you
souls from drear - y paths of sin, paths of sin, Lift them

greet the world with song as thru life you pass a - long, Cheer - ing
let your light so shine that they see the path di - vine, And you
up on high - er plains, where they'll hear the glad re - frains, Of the

CHORUS

those whom you may meet a - long life's way?
wear a pleas - ant smile a - long life's way.
smil - ing band of work - ers on life's way.

Give the
Give the world a

world a bright smile ev - 'ry day, Help - ing some - one
smile each day, Help - ing some - one on life's

Four
A Little History

Many are curious about the history of Southern gospel music. There are a lot of opinions as to where it all started, and as a sort of modern aficionado, I can tell you this: the genre is not that old, and there are some things we can nail down about its roots. Let me tell you what I know, not as a historian (because this is not in any way intended to be an extensive historical document), but as a fellow fan. This is the story from the perspective of one who loves the music, and any omission of significant contributors to its rise and success is totally unintentional.

My hope is that you'll discover where the history of the music intersects your own history—as I did—and that from that you will gain an understanding of why it seems to engender such a visceral response. For instance, I only became aware of the music style as a child growing up in the 1930s and 1940s. I didn't know Southern gospel was fairly new even then. To me it had always been there. To someone growing up in the radio and TV heyday of Southern gospel, the 1950s and 1960s, the style must have seemed as old as the church itself.

Before we started these videos, it may have been that Southern gospel had taken a backseat to all the newer styles of Christian music since the 1960s and 1970s. If our bringing back the legends and introducing some new young people in this category of music helps breathe some fresh life into Southern gospel, that would make me happy.

It's been very gratifying to hear from many of the older "stars" who were in semi-retirement that their phones are ringing again for bookings. That's all the reward I need. Maybe some of this history will reveal why Southern gospel is a style that needs to stay around a few more decades.

Because my role has come to be a catalyst to reunite these people, if I start saying who's best or most legendary, I can offend those I leave out. There have been friendly rivalries, of course, and maybe some petty jealousies over the years. And yet, looking at the field from the perspective of decades—not to mention as a fan and an outsider (which allowed me to contribute as a composer and a catalyst), I've found there truly is a hierarchy of legends that everyone generally agrees upon.

Though some may wish they had been members of some of the biggest and best and best-known groups, they can't deny that those groups paved the way. Baseball has its Yankees and Dodgers; Southern gospel has its Blackwoods and Statesmen. Baseball has its Babe Ruths and Mickey Mantles and Jackie Robinsons; Southern gospel has its Hovie Listers, James Blackwoods, Jake Hesses, Mom and Dad Speers, and Eva Mae LeFevres.

James D. Vaughan, the pioneer of Southern Gospel quartet singing.

But where did it all start? What is convention-style singing? And what is all this you hear people saying on the videos about having learned to read music via the shaped-notes system?

The first major early influence on gospel music—and, many would say, the pioneer of Southern gospel quartet singing—was James D. Vaughan. He was a school teacher and lover of gospel music who had sung in a quartet with three of his brothers.

A turning point for Vaughan came when he attended a music school taught by E. T. Hildebrand. Such schools used an interesting style of teaching. They made use of four individually shaped notes, each shape representing a different note on the scale. Thus a singer could look at the shape of the note and know whether it was fa, sol, la, or mi. One of the earliest styles of shaped-notes music is actually several hundred years old and was called Sacred Harp, named after its most popular songbook. Some who learned this style of music were called "Fasola Folk."

Through the Hildebrand school, James Vaughan learned to sing and to write music. His first compositions were published by Hildebrand-Burnett Publications. He would go on to write hundreds of songs, probably the most well-known being "I Feel Like Traveling On."

In 1900 Vaughan published his first songbook, *Gospel Chimes*. Two years later, when he was thirty-eight years old, he quit teaching school and resettled in Lawrenceburg, Tennessee, to become a full-time music publisher. It was a bold and risky move, but the deeply spiritual and charismatic man with a beaming smile made a quick success of it.

Since the earliest shaped-notes system had just four shaped notes, teaching and writing music was not very precise. Vaughan refined the process to provide for a different shape for all seven notes on the scale.

His songbooks slowly became popular, because the heavily churched South was full of people who loved

V. O. Stamps, founder of the Stamps Music Company, which, along with the Vaughan Music Company, was one of the two early giants of the gospel music field.

to sing praise songs and hymns. Vaughan's had memorable lyrics and interesting tempos, and because of the unique shaped notes, they were easy to sight-read, even for the layperson. Within seven years he was selling songbooks at the rate of about 30,000 a year.

Vaughan's next stroke of marketing genius was to send out a company quartet, the first of which (in 1910) included one of his brothers. James had devised a style of singing where the high tenor sang the alto part

The original Dallas-based Stamps Quartet (standing from l): Jim Gaither (no relation to me), Walter Rippetoe, Bob Bacon, pianist Marion Snider, (seated) V. O. Stamps. For a time this quartet appeared on more sacred song radio programs than any other quartet in America.

usually sung by women. The Vaughan Quartet became the first professional all-male Southern gospel quartet in America. They sang the new songs and sold the new books, doubling sales in one year. By 1912 they were selling 85,000 songbooks a year.

It wasn't long before James Vaughan realized that if a little was good, a lot was better. He sent out more and more quartets, all with slightly different names, to different areas of the South. (By the middle of the 1920s there would be sixteen Vaughan quartets making the rounds of singing conventions and giving concerts in churches.)

In 1911 Vaughan added a School of Music to his enterprises, at first conducting three-to-four-week schools twice a year. By the 1920s he had instituted a five-month session. Students would come from all over

Back east were the LeFevres (from l): Urias (top), Big Jim Waites (r), Eva Mae, and Alphus (with guitar).

The 1952 Weatherford Quartet (from l): (standing) Earl Weatherford, George Younce, Lily Weatherford; (seated) Danny Koker, Les Roberson.

the South, study under some of the leading gospel musicians in the country, and then return to their own locales to teach others to read shaped notes and sing Vaughan songs.

Business was good and Vaughan opened branch offices in four other states, including Texas. One of the key men in the Vaughan organization was V. O. Stamps.

He would serve Vaughan for many years, including running Vaughan's Jacksonville, Texas, branch before building his own songbook company, also stocked with traveling quartets.

An ad for one of those early schools, run by V. O. Stamps for James D. Vaughan, called it "The Annual Texas Session of the Vaughan Modern Normal School of Music." It was to comprise six weeks, beginning November 11, 1923. Tuition for the term was fifteen dollars, books were furnished free, and board was "from five to seven dollars per week."

Private lessons in voice, piano, violin, guitar, and mandolin were offered for from seventy-five cents to a dollar a lesson. The rest of the copy in the ad promised, "We have spared no expense in bringing together the strongest faculty that we could get for this school. We expect it to be the peer of all the good schools heretofore held in Texas.

"These teachers know their business, they are acquainted with conditions here in the field, something that is impossible where men are 'imported' for school work of this kind. There is not a 'has been' in this faculty."

In 1921 Vaughan had cut his first record for the quartet, and in 1922 he built and ran the first radio station (WOAN) in Tennessee, one of few in the United States. There was no commercial radio back then, so WOAN was a financial drain, but it had its benefits nonetheless. Vaughan personally conducted a twelve-piece orchestra and emceed a live nightly broadcast of quartets, trios, duets, and soloists. All this, of course, furthered the cause of Vaughan songbooks throughout the South.

Many of the pioneers of country music and in Southern gospel quartet singing studied at the Vaughan school. The Speer Family and the LeFevre Trio were seen there as early as the 1930s. And if there's one common denominator in the stories of most of the quartet singers of the 1940s and 1950s, it is that they attended one of the singing convention schools and learned to read shaped-notes music.

By the 1940s, the Vaughan and Stamps and later the Stamps-Baxter schools were friendly—and sometimes not so friendly—rivals. They staked out territories where their dozens of quartets would take songbooks, nail down a live daily broadcast on a local radio station, and hold concerts within a 200-mile radius. The quartets would generally sing live on the radio in the morning, promoting their songbooks and announcing their availability for concerts (including where they would be performing that evening). Then they would drive to their concert, sing—sometimes late into the night—and drive all the way back to make it to the radio studio in time for their broadcast the next morning.

At concerts the quartets' primary responsibility to the company paying their salaries was to sell those songbooks. All of us today who travel and minister through music owe some debt to these early groups. It was a hard life. Some prospered more than others, but the history of gospel music is full of starving artists.

They loved it, but even into the 1950s, many struggling groups subsisted on a few dollars a day for meals, virtually living in huge cars that didn't seem so huge when four singers and a pianist had to compete for space on long trips.

Most of the country styles and harmonies you hear today in both secular and Christian music stem from James D. Vaughan's early songbooks or those from his protégé and eventual business competitor, V. O. Stamps and the Stamps-Baxter Music and Printing Company.

Vaughan died in 1941, but his company continued.

V. O. Stamps' original Stamps Quartet broadcast for the first time a regular daily fifteen-minute show on KRLD out of Dallas in 1936, and their theme song was "Give the World a Smile Each Day." It's still a favorite among many traveling groups today.

Give the World a Smile Each Day

Are you giving to the world a smile, sunny smile,
Helping lessen someone's dreary mile, dreary mile?
Do you greet the world with a song as thru life you
*   pass along,*
Cheering those whom you may meet along life's
*   way?*

You may be a shining light today, yes, today,
Pointing souls to heaven's glory way, glory way,
If you let your light so shine that they see the path
*   divine,*
And you wear a pleasant smile along life's way.

Just a bright and sunny smile will win, it will win,
Many souls from dreary paths of sin, paths of sin,
Lift them up on higher plains, where they'll hear
*   the glad refrains,*
Of the smiling band of workers on life's way.

Give the world a smile each day,
Helping someone on life's way;
From the paths of sin bring the wanderers in,
To the Master's fold to stay.
Help to cheer the lone and sad,
Help to make some pilgrim glad,
Let your life so be that all the world may see
The joy of serving Jesus with a smile, a bright
*   sunny smile.*[1]

I didn't know the difference back then, of course, but the two major movements out of which most of these groups came happened to be two very devout sides of the same theological coin.

James D. Vaughan was a Nazarene who came from a holiness/Wesleyan background. V. O. Stamps, who began with Vaughan and then went on his own, was just as deeply spiritual but from more of a Calvinist, Southern Baptist tradition.

When I try to explain theological differences I'm practicing without a license, but at their most basic, these were two different camps. Vaughan emphasized holiness and living a sanctified life, separated from the world. My impression of the teaching of that movement at that time was that the sanctified life was evidenced in the way you dressed (extremely modestly) and if you avoided makeup, contemporary hairstyles, and the like. Basically, they avoided any style that would draw attention to oneself. Dad Speer and the Speer Family were from that branch of the movement.

The other side of the gospel music movement at that time didn't have a problem with a little attention. Often the quartets on the Stamps side of the street wore flashy outfits and were very much into showmanship on the stage. (Later some would complain that the Statesmen, with their fancy suits and pencil-thin mustaches, looked like a bunch of riverboat gamblers.) Their detractors said they were more performers than ministers.

V. O. Stamps was from a Baptist tradition that believed once a person was saved, he or she was always saved. The joke was that such a theology made living on the road pretty good. That's funny only as a

That's my brother Danny (l) and me with our sister, Mary Ann—the first Gaither Trio.

The 1978 Bill Gaither Trio (from l): Me, Gloria, and Gary McSpadden.

joke, because even the most dyed-in-the-wool eternal securitist would never consider his assurance of heaven a license for sin.

While these two groups looked at the Christian life and separation from the world a little differently, they were able to work together and appreciate each other. Neither considered the other apostate or not truly Christian, though they differed on certain distinctives.

The theologies of these men was evidenced in the music they published, and it impacts the church to this day. Those early quartets who traveled for the songbook companies had high tenors and low basses, but their voices, based on the few remaining recordings from those days, sounded older than today's typical quartet. And, generally, they *were* made up of older people, mostly men.

There was a Stamps-Ozark Quartet in Wichita Falls, Texas, that had a young singer by the name of Glen Payne (now a legend with the Cathedrals). My old friend Henry Slaughter played the piano for the Stamps-Ozark Quartet.

In Shenandoah, Iowa, a family group called the Blackwood Brothers represented Stamps-Baxter in the traditional manner. They held concerts, had a radio show, and sold books. Later they would break free of the association with the Stamps company and relocate to Memphis. The original Blackwood Brothers Quartet may have been the most nearly perfect combination of voices in gospel singing history. People who remember that group before tragedy took two of the members often say their sound has never been matched.

V. O. Stamps, while originally broadcasting out of Dallas, also made a deal with a station in Del Rio, Texas, that had a tower just across the Mexican border. Because it was located outside the U.S., the station had no power limits and could be heard as far north as Indiana. That began pushing the borders for Southern gospel.

In 1948 a Stamps-Baxter group called the Dixie Four Quartet moved from Memphis to Indianapolis.

The 1985 Gaither Vocal Band (from l): Larnelle Harris, Gary McSpadden, me, Jon Mohr.

That year a farm boy in Alexandria, Indiana, milking the cows one early morning, heard that group on the radio for the first time. I was captivated.

The Dixie Four became my earliest influence in this kind of music. When they said, "We're singing today from the new Stamps book *Golden Steps*, which you can have for fifty cents," I couldn't wait to put two quarters into the mail. When the book finally arrived, I noticed on the back an ad for the Stamps Quartet News. I ordered that and began to get pictures and stories of people doing this kind of work. So then I'd order more books. That's where I learned of the Statesmen out of Atlanta, probably the most exciting group ever on stage.

When the Dixie Four came to sing at a local school, you better know I was there early. And with the regular news I was getting in the mail, I was being exposed to all the great groups around the country. I was thrilled to find out that a whole bunch of other people were doing the same thing.

My love for Southern gospel was in full swing, and my brother, Danny, sister, Mary Ann, and I listened to the great quartets on the radio whenever we could tune them in. The Weatherfords had a program on a nearby station, and they became another early favorite.

My 78-rpm record collection began in earnest. I bought more songbooks, eight-by-ten glossy pictures, you name it. I gathered all I could afford. My room began to look like a shrine to my favorite quartets.

I badgered my parents into driving to Nashville the next year for Wally Fowler's all-night singing. Once there, I was sure that I would soon see the pearly gates. That event was like heaven for me. I had been baited

The 1992 Gaither Vocal Band (from l): Mark Lowry, Terry Franklin, me, Michael English.

The current Bill Gaither Vocal Band (from l): Jonathon Pierce, Guy Penrod, Mark Lowry, (seated) Bill Gaither.

and lured up till then. But after that night at Ryman, the hook was solidly in, and my life has been nearly all music ever since. I didn't know it was only the second year Fowler had been producing such shows. He had taken the old idea of a churchyard's all-day singing and dinner on the ground and brought it indoors. I had been exposed to a genre of worship and entertainment I could have only imagined before.

I came to know about all the groups and their personnel. I was as fanatical about following them as most kids are about following their favorite sports teams. Danny and Mary Ann and I formed the first Gaither Trio and sang wherever anyone would have us. My dream was to start my own group and then be discovered by one of the great quartets and wind up playing and singing for the Blackwoods or the Statesmen.

I was and still am a sports fan (mostly NBA basketball now), but the heroes of my youth were not the sports stars most young boys worshiped. My heroes were Jake Hess, Hovie Lister, James Blackwood, the Weatherfords, the Speer Family, and the other big groups. Their music kept me busy and kept me out of trouble. I spent every spare minute working, playing, practicing, hoping, dreaming, striving toward my goal.

My problem was that even after all that, I was not good enough. After graduating from high school in 1954 I joined a group called the Pathfinders, and we got to where we were opening for some of the big groups. But we didn't sell many tickets for our own concerts, and though we landed a radio show in a small market, we didn't impress anyone. Deciding to give up my dream and go to college and major in another field was one of the most painful experiences of my life.

Once I started college I finally heard from the Weatherfords, who needed a piano player. But my dad made me fulfill my commitment to college. I studied to become a teacher and kept my hand in the music ministry by becoming a church choir director and writing songs on the side. When we first started the Bill Gaither Trio, we didn't have the three hallmarks of a Southern gospel group. We didn't have a red-hot piano player. We didn't have a high tenor. And we didn't have a low bass. We went with what we had: a songwriter who played a little piano and sang a little bass/baritone, my wife, Gloria, who sang alto, and my brother, Danny, who was a great lead singer, handling the melody. Our style came to be known as "Inspirational." Maybe that's why we were never seen as competition to all those groups and were able in the end to pull them all back together.

As for the way singers have conducted themselves on the road over the years, I have to say there were inconsistencies, as there probably are today. These are people of clay and people who have failed, but they are also people who have asked forgiveness, and God has restored them. In my opinion, our videos are in many cases monuments to the grace of God, restoration, and reconciliation.

If we waited for a totally unflawed group of artists or an unflawed group of preachers or an unflawed group of communicators or leaders in the Christian church, we would probably be a pretty small church. Does this mean there is not a higher standard for Christian leaders? Certainly not. There is a higher standard.

But if a sin is under the blood and in the past, I'm not going to hold it against a person any more than God would hold it against them.

On my very best day I am like anybody else in that room; I'm still just a sinner saved by grace. We are all there only by the grace of God, because we have been redeemed.

While it is painfully true that some sins have more lasting and far-reaching consequences than others, at the end of life, in the perspective of eternity, our standing before God is determined by the work done on the cross on our behalf by the shedding of the blood of Christ. I thank God for that and celebrate that every time I open my mouth to sing. And I am thankful for both James Vaughan and V. O. Stamps, who came from two different theological camps, but who were God's treasures in earthen vessels and used by Him in very special ways.

1940 Blackwood Brothers (from l): pianist Hilton Griswold, Bill Lyles, R.W. Blackwood, James Blackwood, Roy Blackwood.

Five

The Pioneers

What grew from the Vaughan and Stamps empires of the first half of the twentieth century was a musical style that today sees some 2,000 quartet-style groups traveling the country. Some things have changed and evolved, and there have been offshoots, splits, and the usual winnowing process. Here and there you see groups so old-fashioned and traditional that they would have easily fit into one of the stables of traveling quartets sent out by the songbook publishing companies of the 1930s. Glen Payne's and George Younce's Cathedrals are probably the best of the current list of throwback quartets, with their strong lead, rolling bass, tight-harmony tenor and baritone, and a heavy reliance on the keyboard.

But strangely, for as entrenched and well-known as the Cathedrals are, and with the combined experience of more than 100 years of gospel quartet singing between Payne and Younce alone, they are a relatively recent phenomenon. Even the sensational Statesmen date back only to the late 1940s. The Speer Family and the LeFevre Trio date all the way back to the early days of the Vaughan school.

Probably not one individual group has a well that goes as deep as the Blackwoods. James is the only surviving original member. He and Jake Hess are considered the

The Chattanooga-based Baxter Quartet (from l): V. O. Fossett, Mrs. J. R. Baxter Jr., Mrs. V. O. Fossett, J. R. Baxter Jr., and Odie Smith. Mr. Baxter ran the Chattanooga office of the Stamps-Baxter Music and Printing Company and was vice president.

The Daniel Quartet on WSM in Nashville (from l): Wallace Fowler, pianist Albert Williams, Troy Daniel, manager John Daniel, and Carl Rains. The old Stamps-Baxter catalog exulted, "These boys have been singing together for years and are considered one of the best gospel song quartets in the nation."

two most stylistic lead singers the industry ever heard. Like Jake, James is semi-retired, though he still sings occasionally. James's relatives and their descendants still influence much of Southern gospel.

By the late 1940s and early 1950s, the scene was dominated by the Blackwoods and the Statesmen and several interestingly named groups such as the Deep South Stamps-Baxter Quartet, the Daniel Quartet, the Smile-A-While Quartet, The Melody Boys, The Rangers Quartet, the Homeland Harmony Quartet, the Jordanaires, and my first favorites, the Dixie Four. The Jordanaires were one of the first groups to cross over into the ever-exploding country music field, appearing regularly on the Grand Ole Opry on WSM in Nashville.

The heyday of quartet-style singing would come in the 1950s and 1960s, when television expanded the horizons for many groups. The first, in the early 1950s, was the Statesmen's Nabisco show, in which Hovie Lister did his own cracker commercials. The show was nationally syndicated and pushed the fun and excitement of Southern gospel into the rest of the country in a big way. The program was quite popular for a year or two.

In the 1950s the Statesmen and the Blackwoods had a TV show called *Singing Time in Dixie*, which featured them and the Speer Family, as well as other guests.

The origination of the National Quartet Convention (NQC) in 1956 helped solidify the industry. J. D. Sumner was one of the main catalysts behind this event. The NQC was also the center of a lot of controversy as new clashed with old and traditional was threatened by contemporary. Trios and mixed (men and women) groups were even excluded for a time in favor of pure four-man

At the same time, in the late 1940s, the Rangers Quartet was coming on strong (from l):
Denver Crumpler, Arnold Hyles, Walter Leverett, Vernon Hyles.

combos. But now, more than forty years later, most agree that the NQC has brought most of the groups together and provided new opportunities for all.

In the 1960s Les Beasley and the Florida Boys came along with a hit TV program, one of the biggest weekly shows in the history of gospel music—*Gospel Singing Jubilee.*

Les was a bit of a visionary, taking more of an interest in television than any of the other groups back then.

His frequent featuring of the Happy Goodman Family spawned their resurgence. They had started with just Howard Goodman and his sisters in the 1940s. Now, with his wife, Vestal, and his two brothers, Sam and Rusty, they were back in a big way. The *Gospel Singing Jubilee* show ran more than a decade.

Another popular and long-running nationally syndicated TV show in the 1960s and 1970s was *The Caravan,* which included the LeFevres, the Blue Ridge

In 1948 the Dixie Four Quartet program on WIBC, Indianapolis caught my attention as I milked the cows. From left:
Gene Lowery, Melvin Doss, Shorty Green, Olen "Honey" Dunn, (seated) Frankie Collins.

The Gospel Singing Caravan (TV program) chorus: The LeFevres, the Prophets, the Blue Ridge, and the Johnson Sisters.

Quartet when George Younce was with them, the Prophets, the Johnson Sisters, and many others.

One of the things you'll notice in the historical pictures of the different groups is that the personnel seem to be in a constant state of flux. You'll find Glen Payne pictured in several different groups. The same with J. D. Sumner, Denver Crumpler, Jake Hess, George Younce, and several others. It was not unusual for a group that stayed in business for more than a decade to have an alumni list of several dozen singers.

One of my favorite things to do, but which I don't get much time for anymore, is to hear the stories of the old days from the men who pioneered the industry for the rest of us. These are always stories of humble beginnings, devout faith, little churches, starving artists, and the hand of God in the midst of trial and tragedy. And yet every story is different.

I want to begin with James Blackwood for several reasons. He goes back farther than most, yet his story is in many ways typical of many. He seemed to grow up with the century, and his is a story of success and failure, the heights of popularity, and yet also nearly unspeakable loss and grief.

If there is one name synonymous with Southern gospel music, it is James Blackwood's. Some might argue that Hovie Lister was as good a quartet master and promoter and businessman. Others might say Jake Hess was a more stylistic lead singer. But none will argue that this slight little man with the distinctive, melodic voice isn't the last surviving dean of Southern gospel.

James has, and always has had, a distinctive style and class. He always dressed well and spoke well and carried himself with dignity, just short of being aloof. This was more shyness and gentleness than ego, though he had much he could have been proud of.

I'll never forget in 1965 when I took my mother to the National Quartet Convention in Memphis and found the auditorium sold out. I was a young songwriter with few credits then, but I sought out James and asked if he could help. Not only did he find us a pair of tickets, but he also ushered us all the way up into the balcony and made sure we got settled in. Later he came back to check on us and make sure we were all right and enjoying the show. That was pretty big of a man who could have just as easily shuttled us off to someone else.

Lots of stories and legends surround the history of the Blackwood Brothers Quartet, and their story has been told by many, including James himself. But for the purpose of this book James did us the honor of starting from scratch and dredging up the memories anew.

Following is his brief personal memoir through the lens of nearly eighty years, millions of miles, and more than his share of grief and heartache. You'll agree, I think, that James considers the journey worth it all.

Our family was very poor and lived on a sharecropper farm near the Choctaw County seat of Ackerman, Mississippi, where I was born, August 4, 1919. I was the fourth child and the third of three boys. Roy was the oldest, nearly nineteen by the time I came along. Doyle was already eight, and my parents were in their forties. In fact, Roy presented me with a nephew, R. W., when I was

The Florida Boys (from l): (at the piano) Derrell Stewart, Cory Cook, Les Beasley, Glenn Allred, Billy Todd.

barely two years old. We had a sister, Lena, born in 1903, who also raised a musical family. My father and aunt played fiddles in the Blackwood String Band before the turn of the century, so the music gene ran deep.

Ours was a Christian home, for which I will always be grateful. I've always said that I would rather be raised in a home as poor and humble as ours with Christ there than to live in the finest mansion without God.

One of my earliest memories is seeing my little mother go for her private devotions each morning. After doing the breakfast dishes and sweeping the floor and making the beds, she would get her Bible and make her way down to the garden fence. There she would kneel before her open Bible, reading, then singing (usually "Close to Thee" or "O How I Love Jesus"), and then praying aloud.

You can't imagine the impression that made on a small boy. That seemed like holy ground to me, and when Mama spoke of her love for God, I knew she meant it and that she maintained the relationship.

Every evening after dinner, when the sun went down and the kerosene lamps came on, the family would gather around the fireplace. Mama or Papa would read from the Bible, and then we would all kneel and pray.

When I was about seven years old, Doyle, who was already fifteen, bought a mandolin. I quickly learned to sing alto to his lead, and we copied the style of singing we had been exposed to in church meetings and revivals. People sang out of Vaughan shaped-note songbooks.

One day my dad's brother, my Uncle Remer, came to see us all the way from Jackson, Tennessee. "Doyle," he said, "they tell me you and James sing together. Let me hear you."

We were thrilled to sing for anybody, we loved it so much, so we did a mini-concert for Uncle Remer. He looked delighted. He told Mama and Papa, "There's a singing at the courthouse in Jackson next Sunday, and I'd like to take the boys to sing there."

The Stamps All-Star Quartet, 1949, (from l): Roger Clark, Jack Taylor, Clyde Garner, Glen Payne, (seated) Haskell Mitchell.

V. O. Stamps's brother Frank and the Shreveport-based Stamps Quartet (from l): Aubrey Lowe, Roy Wheeler, Frank Stamps, Wilken Bacon, and pianist Lawrence Ivey. They were available for personal appearances "anywhere within 200 miles of Shreveport," and Frank Stamps was billed as "one of the most successful quartet managers in radio."

I could hardly believe my ears, I was so excited. But Mama said, "James doesn't have clothes nice enough to go to something like that."

"Don't you worry about that," Uncle Remer said. "I'll get him some clothes."

It was fun just to get to ride in a car! We didn't even own one. Uncle Remer drove Doyle and me about 175 miles to Jackson, and sure enough he took me downtown and bought me a sport coat, trousers, shirt, tie, and shoes. Boy, did I feel dressed up!

That Sunday at the singing I stood on a chair next to Doyle and sang. We were a hit and I got my first taste of enthusiastic applause by a big crowd. This was fun!

A quartet there who had a radio program on a local station asked us to sing with them on the air that afternoon. I wasn't even ten years old yet and didn't realize that this would be my first of many thousands of times to sing on the radio.

When I was about ten, Doyle and I heard that a man named Vardiman Ray of the Hartford (Arkansas) Music

was coming to the Clear Springs Baptist Church, about three miles from our home, to teach a singing school out of shaped-note books. We wanted to go so bad we could taste it, but tuition was three dollars each for the ten-night school, and we didn't have anything close to that.

A few days later, after we had resigned ourselves to the fact that there was no hope of going, Mama presented us with three dollars each and told us we could ride the mule to the school every evening after chores. We had no idea where she came up with that sum of money until someone finally told us she had sold some of her chickens.

I loved the music so much that I just drank in everything that school had to offer. Mr. Ray drew the shaped notes on the blackboard, taught us which was which and how to recognize them, and then would drill us by pointing at them randomly. I caught on quickly and my little unchanged voice seemed to be able to find just the right pitches. It was 1929 and I was only ten years old, but I believe I learned the rudiments of ear training and sight-reading during that week and a half.

Frank Stamps, V. O.'s brother, who took over the Stamps-Baxter Music Company when V. O. died in August of 1940. In 1946 Frank would pull away from Stamps-Baxter and start his own Stamps Music Company, moving down the street and becoming a competitor to the company his brother had founded.

Mr. Ray was impressed with Doyle and me and asked if we wanted to sing in a quartet with him and a local bass named Gene Catledge. He didn't have to ask twice. Mr. Ray sang lead, Doyle baritone, and me alto. Our first time to sing together was at an all-day singing at Concord Baptist Church, five miles south of Ackerman. I remember that a new songbook had come out just that day, so Mr. Ray took us out under a tree where we sight-read some new songs and then went right up and performed them. I was getting incredible training for a little boy, with no idea how it would benefit my life as a career quartet man.

We decided to call ourselves the Choctaw County Jubilee Singers, quite a name for a young quartet.

My oldest brother, Roy, was by now a minister who pastored churches all over the country. In each church he had a quartet where he sang lead and his son, R. W. (my two-years-younger nephew) would sing alto, and two men from the church would sing baritone and bass.

One Christmas he and his family came back to Ackerman to visit, and he brought a Victrola and several 78-rpm records of gospel quartets. There was Frank Stamps and his All-Star Quartet, the Owens Brothers, and the Vaughan Quartet. I had never heard phonograph records before, let alone professional quartets singing the music I loved.

I learned to sing "after beats" listening to Mr. Stamps's quartet sing V. O. Stamps's composition "He Bore It All." I couldn't know what a huge influence V. O. Stamps would have on our lives.

For the next few years, Doyle and I continued to sing with Mr. Ray, and I continued to learn much about ministering, performing, and reading music. My desire to spend my life singing gospel music was instilled during that time and had a profound impact on me.

Probably the crucial turning point in my life came in 1934 when I was fifteen and my oldest brother Roy moved back to our area. Doyle and I immediately hooked up with Roy and his son R. W., who would quickly become more a brother than a nephew to me, and formed what we called the Blackwood Brothers Quartet. Doyle played the guitar and sang bass. Roy sang lead. R. W. sang alto and I sang the baritone part an octave higher because our voices hadn't changed yet.

Homeland Harmony (from l): Connor B. Hall, James R. McCoy, Paul Stringfellow, Big Jim Waites, and Wally Varner (at piano).

We sang anywhere people would have us. We would travel through the countryside in Roy's old car, find some school, and approach the principal. We'd offer the school a percentage of the receipts (charging ten cents for adults and five for children) if they'd let us sing in the school. The school buses would bring the families and the kids in at night for the concert, and that's one of the ways we started.

When things got real rough for us in 1935, we had to break up. We had been working all day and trying to sing in the evenings, but pay was scarce, and Roy could barely support his family. He took a church in Fort Worth, and of course his son R. W. went with him. That left Doyle and me, until Doyle left to join the Homeland Harmony Quartet. For two years I prayed that we would somehow get back together and make things work.

In 1937 my prayers were answered. Roy and R. W. moved back, and as soon as Doyle heard that, he came back home too. We tried the traveling and singing business again, this time determined to stay at it no matter what. That resolve was sometimes the only thing that

James Blackwood.

Glen Payne of the Cathedrals, one of the greatest lead singers in the gospel field, singing with Guy Penrod of the Gaither Vocal Band.

The Cathedrals (from l): George Younce, Glen Payne, Scott Fowler, Ernie Haase, and Roger Bennett at the piano.

Ira Stanphill is one of Gloria's and my favorite writers. He wrote such great songs as "I Know Who Holds Tomorrow," "Room at the Cross," "Mansion Over the Hilltop," "Suppertime," and many others.

The Stamps Quartet (from l): Rick Strickland, Ed Enoch, Ed Hill, and J. D. Sumner.

Larry Gatlin of the famed Gatlin Brothers, reuniting with his old friends, Jim Murray (with whom Larry sang during his short stint with the Imperials), Ben Speer, and me.

*Naomi Sego Reader, former alto of
Naomi and the Segos.*

*Audrey Mieir, who's no longer with us, writer of such
great songs as "His Name Is Wonderful," "It Matters to
Him About You," and many others.*

*The legendary Hovie
Lister giving a good
report on his health at a
taping in Indiana.*

The Nelons: Jerry Thompson, Amy Roth, Kelly Nelon Thompson, and father Rex.

Singer Dony McGuire (formerly of the Downings), mother-in-law songwriter Dottie Rambo, and Dottie's daughter, Reba Rambo McGuire.

Calvin Newton, who was welcomed back into the fold after falling away, doing prison time, then seeing God rebuild his life and music ministry.

Here I am with Alvin Slaughter, who was one of the primary soloists with the Brooklyn Tabernacle choir before going solo.

Brock Speer, one of the most respected
men in gospel music today.

Rosa Nell, Mary Tom, and Ben Speer with the Gatlins.

The Florida Boys (from l): Buddy Liles, Glenn Allred, Les Beasley,
and Billy Hodges.

The Couriers (from l):
Phil Enloe, Neil Enloe,
and Duane Nicholson.

The Isaacs, a family group, provide a fantastic new bluegrass sound in gospel music.

Jessy Dixon, already popular in the African-American community, is becoming a favorite in the Southern gospel field.

John Starnes of Georgia, one of the favorite tenors among fans of our videos.

Lynda Tait Randle, a young soloist and sister of Michael Tait of D. C. Talk.

Babbie Mason of Jackson, Michigan, singing, "All Rise."

Squire Parsons, writer of the famous "Sweet Beulah Land," was with the Kingsmen and is now a wonderful soloist.

Jimmy Jones, originally with the Rangers Quartet out of Texas and then with the famous LeFevres out of Georgia. Jimmy is known for his dramatic readings.

Geraldine and Ricky, having a lot of fun at my expense.

Aaron Wilburn, formerly with the Goodman Family, is a wonderful songwriter who co-wrote "It Won't Rain Always" and "It's Beginning to Rain" with Gloria and me.

Newcomer Guy Penrod, who is winning the hearts of everyone as a member of the Gaither Vocal Band.

Mary Tom (Speer) Reid, beloved member of the Speer Family.

Janet Paschal, who was introduced to the gospel music field with the Nelons, is now a soloist.

Larnelle Harris is one of the best-loved gospel singers of all time and was at one time a member of the Gaither Vocal Band.

A familiar pose of J. D. Sumner, cupping his ear. Bass singers often do this. Because they don't sing as loudly as other singers, this allows them to hear their notes better.

Vestal and Howard Goodman, Mr. and Mrs. Gospel Music of the Gaither Video series.

The legendary Fairfield Four: Robert Hamlett, Wilson Waters, Joe Rice, James Hill, and Isaac Freeman.

Soloist Terry Blackwood (son of original Blackwood Brothers member Doyle Blackwood and nephew of James Blackwood).

Lillie Knauls, formerly of the Edwin Hawkins Singers, who had a gold record with the hit "O Happy Day."

The Talleys: Debra and Roger with Kirk.

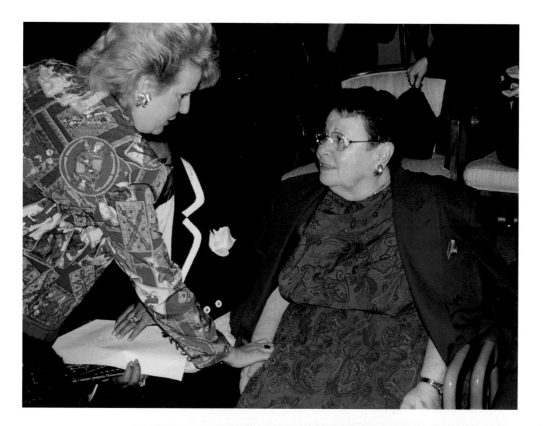

*Publisher Judy Spencer with
the late Doris Akers, writer of
"Sweet, Sweet Spirit" and
"Sweet Jesus."*

Moments of praise.

Homecoming Friends

kept us going. When the first 250-watt radio station came to Kosciusko, Mississippi (about forty miles from our home), we wanted to sing on the air. The station was not on a network and had few records, so most anyone who could carry a tune or pick a banjo could get on. We believed we were better than what we heard, so one Sunday morning we drove on over there.

We found the radio station in the back room of an old house, the entire operation being run by one man. He agreed to put us on for fifteen minutes, but as soon as we began, the phone started ringing. At the end of our time the man was still on the phone and motioned for us to keep singing. We realized all those calls were people trying to order our music or ask for more of our songs.

Fifteen minutes later the same thing happened, and we didn't get off the air until we had sung for an hour and a quarter. The man asked us to come and sing for a half hour every Sunday, and we did that for several months.

Of course we weren't making any money in those days, so the four of us got a contract to cut timber for a saw mill. We practiced our singing while chopping down trees and cutting them into logs.

Roy's old car really began to suffer after hundreds of miles throughout the area. The brakes were gone, so whoever was driving had to plan ahead. There was a lot of downshifting and feathering those brakes

Shorty Bradford was lead singer of the Homeland Harmony Quartet, which included the great writer Lee Roy Abernathy. Shorty's wife, Jean Bradford, is a wonderful singer/songwriter in her own right.

to get the thing stopped. One day a mule ran out in front of the car and Roy downshifted twice before slowing enough to throw it in reverse and just miss the beast.

At a singing contest at Union School near our home, we entered both the quartet division and the duet division (Doyle and me). We won both divisions and went home with a twenty-four-pound bag of flour, a bucket of lard, and other assorted groceries.

We announced our availability for concerts on our Sunday radio program and we also saved up and bought some horn-shaped loudspeakers to mount on the car. We would drive around singing and announcing concerts. One man told us that the first time he heard us, he ran into the house and told his wife he thought it was the end of the world. He was convinced he'd heard Gabriel blowing his horn!

In Noxapater, Mississippi, we netted twenty-seven dollars for one night's work, and I got to thinking that if we

The Blackwood Brothers c. 1950: Jackie Marshall (top), Bill Shaw (l), Bill Lyles, James Blackwood, and R.W. Blackwood.

could average that, we'd be rich in no time. We soon decided to make our big break and move to Jackson. It was a bigger market with a popular morning radio program. We weren't paid to sing on the radio, but it opened a lot of opportunities for us.

We were invited to the Mississippi State Singing Convention in the Jackson armory building and were actually on the program with Frank Stamps and his famous All-Star Quartet. We had heard them only on Victrola records, so it was a thrill to see them live.

We must have impressed him too, because he immediately called his brother, V. O. and encouraged him to keep an eye on us. That would really benefit us in the future. Meanwhile, two rooms in the little upstairs King Hotel on Capitol Street became our home. Roy and his wife Susie and their toddler Cecil lived in one room while Doyle, R. W., and I lived in the other. Our income was so meager that we barely scraped up enough for fifteen-cent breakfasts and five-cent burgers for lunch. We had graduated to a 1935 Ford, which we drove until it wouldn't run anymore and the finance company came and got it.

It was clear people enjoyed our sound and our performances, and many told us they were blessed by our ministry. We wanted to keep on, but we didn't know what we were going to do. Without a car, we were finished. We asked a lot of people to lend us the money, and no one would.

KMA, Shenandoah, Iowa, the Blackwood Brothers Quartet (standing from l): Roy Blackwood, James Blackwood, R. W. Blackwood, and Doyle Blackwood; (seated) pianist Hilton Griswold. "... considered among the finest entertainers in radio."

A young man in the radio station overheard us talking about our predicament and graciously offered to co-sign a loan for us so we could get a decent vehicle. We bought a good used 1938 two-door Ford, and we were back in business. If that young man had not helped us out, we might have folded our tents and headed back to Ackerman before our careers ever got off the ground.

One day we were at an all-day singing and dinner on the ground at a little village called Weathersby, on highway 49 about thirty-five miles south of Jackson. I saw the prettiest young woman from the stage and tried to make eyes at her and flirt with her, but I was getting no response. During a break I went out and around the back

The Jordanaires, 1952, (from l): first tenor Bill Matthews, baritone and arranger Monty Matthews, bass Culley Holt, pianist and tenor Gordon Stoker, and second tenor Bobby Hubbard.

and came in behind her. She was holding a "Glory Dawn" songbook and I could see her name on the front: Miriam Grantham.

I recognized her name immediately, and though my heart was racing and I felt weak-kneed, I managed, "Say, didn't I get a song request letter from you at the radio station recently?" That broke the ice, and suddenly I was talking to this beautiful high school student. (I was only two years older than she was.) Eventually she invited the quartet to her parents' home for a meal and, of course, had to ride with us so we could find it. She later admitted

that she had put her name on the songbook on purpose so I might notice.

Her mother proved to be a great cook, and as Mim's and my courtship began, I spent a lot of time eating at her place. The other single guys in the quartet had girlfriends too, so we traded using the car on off days. Once when I wanted to see Mim and it wasn't my turn for the car, I took a bus to see her, taking only enough money for fare both ways.

When I arrived, starved for a great meal, Mim told me her mother was under the weather and that we were to go into town and eat. I figured I could afford Mim's meal but no more if I wanted to keep enough change for the ride back home. I insisted I wasn't hungry, but my stomach growled and my mouth watered as Mim ate. When the bill came I tried to pay, but she said, "No, James. Mama gave me enough for both of us!"

I could have eaten! For years Mim cried whenever she heard me tell that story, ashamed that she had eaten while I was hungry. But it was my own pride that had cost me a good meal.

In late 1938 the Blackwood Brothers were asked to audition for a two-program spot on a 10,000-watt station in Shreveport, Louisiana. It seemed a great opportunity, and we won. We moved to Louisiana, and our base of operations really widened. We had more exposure and traveled farther every day to sing. Mr. V. O. Stamps heard us sing on the radio and soon offered to make us The Blackwood Brothers-Stamps Quartet, providing a car and income as we represented his company. We had gone

from starvation to a fairly respectable situation almost overnight, but we never forgot who we were and who we weren't. We knew God had his hand on our ministry.

After a seven-month courtship, Mim and I were married May 4, 1939 in the same ceremony with Doyle and his bride, Lavez Hawkins. (I bought a thirty-two dollar wedding ring at five dollars down and five dollars a month, and Mim still wears it today, nearly 60 years later.) Within a year R. W. married too, so we were all family men.

In the spring of 1940 V. O. Stamps asked us to relocate to Iowa. We hardly knew where that was. It might as well have been China to us southern boys. We hated to leave Shreveport and the 50,000-watt radio station, but we trusted Mr. Stamps and wanted to do whatever he needed.

We were strange to the Midwest and it was strange to us. But we quickly caught on and were traveling hundreds of miles every day, singing almost every night and doing three radio shows a day, two of them live. Sleep became a precious commodity. I had it perfectly timed. I set my alarm

The 1955 Jordanaires, who stayed together without a personnel change until Hoyt Hawkins died in 1982 (from l): Neal Matthews, Gordon Stoker, Hoyt Hawkins, Ray Walker.

Mr. and Mrs. Albert Brumley. Albert is best known for "I'll Fly Away,"
"Turn Your Radio On," "If We Never Meet Again This Side of Heaven,"
"Jesus Hold My Hand," and his list is just about endless. He was one
of the first really commercial writers in the gospel field and is a member
of the Country Music Hall of Fame.

tening audience at a million people in twenty-seven states and three Canadian provinces.

We got a raise to forty dollars a week each and a brand-new 1941 Olds. We finally felt we had arrived. Despite feeling cramped in that otherwise roomy car (five full-grown men just don't sleep comfortably on the road), we enjoyed our lives and ministry.

In December of 1941 the Japanese attacked Pearl Harbor, and the end of our nice situation came into view. By spring we knew we would have to disband until the war was over, what with rationing and all the rest. Amazingly, we all relocated to California and worked in defense plants during the day, still getting together and singing here and there in the evenings. Eventually Doyle fell ill and moved back to Mississippi. R. W. was drafted. Roy was depressed about that and went home too, to be close to Mama and Papa and Doyle. I was

for seven-twenty-two, jumped into my clothes, ran to the car, and walked into the studio just as Hilton Griswold, our new pianist, was playing the introduction for our first song.

In a competition with the other Stamps quartets, we sold songbooks left and right. When it was all over, we had sold more than all the other groups combined. Mr. Stamps put our picture on the cover of his newspaper and allowed us to offer it free for two weeks. Ten thousand people requested it, causing the radio station to estimate our lis-

the only original member left, but Hilton Griswold and I were able to get together with a few others to keep things going until we could be reunited.

On the first day of 1946, with Californian Don Smith as our bass, Hilton Griswold at the piano, me on lead, Roy at tenor, and R. W. singing baritone, we were back on radio station KMA in Shenandoah, Iowa. I missed Doyle.

We severed our relationship amicably with the Stamps organization. V. O. Stamps had died and we wanted to

market our own books anyway. We began cutting and marketing records, recording them in the radio station.

In 1947, when Don Smith went back to California, we picked up Bill Lyles as our new bass singer. He was a tall, handsome young man with a beautifully smooth voice and a wonderful smile. He came highly recommended, and many still put him at or near the top of any list of the best quartet basses ever. We persuaded Doyle to rejoin us and we had a unique sound that we perfected, rehearsing every chance we got.

During those final years of the decade of the 1940s we continued to travel widely by car and sing almost every day and night over the radio and in concerts. Twice we were in bad car wrecks, once almost losing Hilton and another time seeing a woman killed when the car she was in collided with ours. At times I wondered if it was worth going on, but I had to remind myself that God had His hand on us and that we were doing what He wanted us to do.

We became so popular and had so much going that we actually brought in enough personnel to run the office and put two entirely separate quartets on the road. It was all I could do to juggle everything I had in the air.

We sang on TV for the first time in Omaha in December of 1948. We became as widely known and successful as we could imagine, and I started to feel that we might have saturated our own market. Within two years we would move back to the south, settling in Memphis to try to plow new ground.

Alden Toney sang with the Blackwoods in the early 1950s and with his brothers in Detroit.

THE PIONEERS

The McDuff Brothers are a good example of how hair and clothing styles change over the years. As children (from l): John, Colman, and Roger. Outdoors (from l) it's Colman, Roger, and John. And [opposite page] with Lorne Matthews (far right) 1970, (from l) John, Roger, and Colman.

Hilton Griswold would not return with us. After having been a most crucial and integral part of our ministry for ten years, he felt called to stay in Iowa and become a minister. I knew he was doing what God wanted him to, but I didn't know if we could ever replace him.

I called around to people I trusted and everyone seemed to recommend a young man named Jackie Marshall. With all the praise he got, I hired him sight unseen and met him for the first time right before one of our last broadcasts in Iowa. He looked like he was fourteen years old, a little bitty fellow who made me wonder what I had done. Until he sat down at the keys. He became one of the most popular quartet pianists ever, and we were blessed to get him.

By 1952 we had put together what I believe, and many other people in our industry believe, was the best quartet sound possible. Bill Lyles was the consummate bass, smooth as silk. R. W. is still considered the best baritone ever to step to the mike. I was singing lead, and our new tenor, Bill Shaw, had a beautifully trained voice that worked perfectly with the rest of us. (He remains my favorite all-time tenor, no disrespect to Rosie Rozell and some of the other greats.) With Jackie Marshall on the piano we finally had the sound I had only dreamed about for years.

We had become an instant success on the radio in Memphis and we turned down many more engagements than we could have accepted. The Statesmen Quartet, under Hovie Lister, was an exciting group that we both competed with and worked with in many joint ventures.

The only problem was that we were wearing ourselves too thin. We were venturing into business, transcripting radio shows, getting into TV, selling records and songbooks and sheet music, booking our own schedules, all the while traveling everywhere in seven-passenger luxury cars that might have been fine for fewer than five people.

We were all exhausted and it was beginning to show. Maybe audiences were unaware that we were not up to par, but we knew, and we began to discuss solutions. Finally R. W. and I came to the conclusion that we needed to look into a new mode of transportation. It would be revolutionary, but as soon as we thought of it, we believed it would be our answer.

An airplane.

A few of us had worked near planes during the war, and both R. W. and Bill Lyles were fascinated by the prospect of learning to fly and navigate. We bought a small plane, then a bigger one, and finally a beautiful new twin-engine Beechcraft. Now that was living!

We were more relaxed and rested, and we performed better than ever. We couldn't imagine life improving until we got a call from New York late in the spring of 1954, asking if we wanted to try out for the *Arthur Godfrey Talent Scouts Show*. It was the top rated TV show of 1954.

"Would I?" I shouted. "Just tell me when and where!"

I was so excited I could hardly tell the others about it. The thought of not being selected never crossed our minds. We

Jessy Dixon.

The original Singing Wills Family (front row, from l): Betty, Lou Wills Hildreth, and Norma Jo.
(Back row, from l): Bob, Calvin.

believed if we could audition, we'd be chosen to compete on the show. We flew our Beechcraft to New York, did well, were enthusiastically accepted, and were told to come back for our live appearance on the night of June 12, 1954.

It was one thing to be the first gospel quartet to appear on nationwide television. That should have been enough. But we didn't want to just compete. We also wanted to win. The winner would appear the next four mornings on Mr. Godfrey's CBS radio and television simulcast. We thought that would be the best opportunity to represent the Lord.

We looked forward to our chance on the *Arthur Godfrey Talent Scouts* TV show as we had never looked forward to an appearance before.[1]

The new singing Hayes Family from Boone, North Carolina, who are very good (back row from l): Janet Hayes Haas, Mylon and Sharon Hayes, (front) Lucy and Howard Hayes.

Larnelle Harris.

(from l) Carolyn, Louise, and Jean Bradford today.

The Blackwood Brothers c. 1954 (from l): Bill Shaw, James Blackwood,
Cecil Blackwood, J. D. Sumner, and Jackie Marshall.

Six
Clanton

The name of this chapter is the name of a city in Alabama that chills any devotee of gospel quartet music. It is the site of a tragedy nearly forty-five years ago that still reverberates in our industry. I can see the pain in James Blackwood's eyes sometimes to this day. Even in his late seventies, James is a bright, peppy performer with a bounce in his step and an enthusiastic smile. Yet every triumph, every joy is tempered with a desolate feeling of terrible loss that adds a solemn patina to the canvas of his ministry. There is a maturity and reality and deeper meaning behind his every lyric, tune, performance, and conversation—all because of what happened in Clanton, Alabama in 1954.

I'll let him pick up the story:

Television was still in its infancy, but still millions had TV sets in their homes all over America. We knew that on the *Arthur Godfrey Talent Scouts* program in New York we would be singing before more people than we ever had in auditoriums, multiplied thousands of times. We were nervous. I knew I was, and I could see it written on R. W.'s and Jackie's and the two Bills's faces. My hands were sweaty as I prayed, "Lord, I know You're in this. Bless the people who hear us. Use us. We want You to be glorified."

I tried to regulate my breathing as we waited in our new, matching suits with sharp contrasting pocket kerchiefs and ties. Then, just like that, we were announced and the five of us ran onto the stage. Jackie slid behind the keyboard and we hit the first notes of "Have You Talked to the Man Upstairs?"

Sometimes you have a sense when something is going well. We had enough experience to cover and make do when we were off, but that wasn't a problem that night. We smiled, we stayed with each other, we were hitting the pitches and the harmonies. We weren't too loud or too soft, too slow or too fast. Jackie was wailing away at the piano and we were cooking, playing to the studio audience and Mr. Godfrey as much as to those huge, funny looking box cameras that we knew represented millions of viewers.

When we finished, the audience erupted and Mr. Godfrey was grinning broadly as he too applauded.

At the end of the show he asked each participant back to do a tiny sample of their performance as the audience reacted. It was plain to everyone. We had won.

It's hard to describe the feeling of being on top of the world. We were excited and proud, yet humble and grateful too. We were young men—R. W., 32 and I, 34—but old enough not to let this go to our heads. We had worked awfully hard for a long time, and it was as if God had given us this gift to bless us for being faithful and obedient to Him.

As soon as we got back to our hotel we thanked God for His goodness and kindness. After calls to and from home and many well-wishers, we tried in vain to get a

James Blackwood.

The Blackwood Brothers and the McGuire Sisters pictured in a CBS studio in New York as they joined together to sing "Lead Me To That Rock," on Godfrey's Morning Progrom.

good night's sleep so we would be ready for Mr. Godfrey's two-hour radio/TV simulcast the next four mornings.

Things had come together perfectly, and it seemed we were made for that show. Every number was a hit and well-received, and telegrams poured in. RCA Victor saw their recording of our "Have You Talked to the Man Upstairs?" shoot into the top ten of the pop charts. On the last morning we sang "His Hand in Mine," and the audience seemed hushed and moved. It was such a privilege to sing an overt testimony song like that! I stole a glance at Mr. Godfrey, and he had tears in his eyes.

His Hand in Mine

You may ask me how I know my Lord is real;
You may doubt the things I say and doubt the way I feel.
But I know He's real today; He'll always be.
I can feel His hand in mine, and that's enough for me.

Other friends that I love so may pass me by;
Other friends may never see the teardrops in my eye;

Other friends may never know the pain I bear.
Every tear He wipes away, and every heartache shares.

I will never walk alone; He holds my hand.
He will guide each step I take, and if I fall,
I know He'll understand.

'Til the day He tells me why He loves me so,
I can feel His hand in mine; that's all I need to know.
When the time shall come to leave this world behind,
I will walk that lonesome valley with His hand in mine.[1]

When we flew back south and resumed our personal appearances, we were astounded by the response. We were met by big crowds at airports and every venue was sold out. We received standing ovations just coming out on stage. All of us were careful to express our thanks to God and to remind the people that all the glory must go to Him. But I can't deny it was the greatest feeling in the

R. W. Blackwood (l) and Bill Lyles in the ill-fated cockpit of the Blackwood Brothers' plane.

world, being loved and appreciated by the audiences everywhere we went. It was as if we could do no wrong.

We were at the top and the sky was the limit.[2]

Many of us in the gospel music field, including Gloria and me, know how heady those days can be when it seems everything is working for you and the world loves you. It's important, of course, to never take yourself too seriously, because fame and adoration can be so fleeting.

It's not difficult to imagine, however, how much fun that period had to be for James and R. W. and the three others. They were the toast of the gospel music world. They'd won the big contest, been on national radio and TV, had a top-ten best-seller, owned their own plane, and were performing as never before.

Rare vintage film of that period shows a quartet that had meshed as none other before or since. They were happy, they were sharp, and it showed.

James picks up the story:

The notes came sharp and clear. The pitches were true. The harmony was sweet. We were singing better than we ever had before.

June 29, 1954, thirteen days after our last morning appearance on the Godfrey show, we flew into Gulfport, Mississippi for a sing. It was a hot night and we sweat through our suits, but things went exceptionally well. In fact I'd have to say we hit a peak. It was more than something special as everything clicked and the performance was as perfect as we could imagine. The audience responded. People were blessed and so were we.

We often ate our dinner after our evening concert, and that night it was just the five of us. Things had been going so well that it was hard to imagine them getting any better. R. W., though he was technically my nephew, was closer to me than any of my brothers had ever been, because they were all so much older. We reminisced that night about starting out twenty years before, the two of us the only ones who had been with the Blackwoods from the beginning.

Bill Shaw, Bill Lyles, and Jackie Marshall enjoyed our stories from the early days, and after dinner the five of us walked on the beach there in Mississippi. I remember telling R. W., "I don't know what's coming next, but it must be going to be spectacular. I can't believe how God has moved. I'm holding my breath waiting for the next miracle."

R. W., who had just rejoined us after a quick trip to Memphis where he saw young Cecil and his wife Doris's new baby, Mark, was telling us all about the proud new parents. Cecil, Roy's boy who had been a preschooler

when we were scratching out a living in Jackson, Mississippi, fifteen years before, had begun singing in a church quartet back home.

Early the next morning we flew from Gulfport, Mississippi, to Clanton, Alabama, where we would sing at noon and in the evening the last night of the five-day Chilton County Peach Festival in the hangar right at the dirt airstrip. The Statesmen would be joining us, and though we had a friendly rivalry, we always enjoyed being with them. It was going to be good to see Hovie Lister, Big Chief Wetherington, Jake Hess, and the rest.

I had long been impressed by R. W.'s ability to fly a plane. He had been a quick study, and he and Bill always sat in the cockpit, R. W. handling the flying and Bill the navigating. The dirt strip at Clanton was only 2,500 feet long, a little short for a twin Beechcraft, so R. W. looped the plane when we reached the end of the field. We would sing a few songs at noon, visit the town of Clanton in the afternoon, do the concert with the Statesmen that night, and then fly back to Memphis. Though the airstrip was unlighted, we knew folks in the audience would be glad to line the runway with their cars and shine their headlights until we were back in the air.

We emerged from the plane at about eleven that morning to an unusually hot and clear Alabama day. After our brief luncheon appearance, we visited town where we were gratified to be recognized by so many who had seen us on the Godfrey show. We were shown around Clanton by a local teenager, Johnny Ogburn, son of the promoter of the Peach Festival. He was a fan and fascinated by planes, so he stuck with us all day.

Late in the afternoon, not long before we were scheduled for our concert at the hangar, R. W. suggested that we go back to the airstrip early. "I'd like to take the plane up before dark so I can see how much room I've got for the takeoff tonight." R. W. had always been a careful pilot, never shortcutting his preflight checklist and all. We trusted him with our lives.

Just before dusk we got to the airstrip, where a few of the Statesmen milled about and thousands of others enjoyed the Peach Festival and were beginning to make their way to the hangar for the concert. Some of the Statesmen had flown with us before, but they didn't have the stomach for it and stuck with their big, seven-passenger car.

R. W. and Bill boarded the plane for the test flight and Johnny Ogburn talked his way on too. The rest of us backed off and watched as R. W. went through his routine and then fired up the engines. The blunt-nosed Beechcraft shot down the runway and hurled itself into the air. R. W. began to circle and I knew young Johnny must be having the time of his life. It would be just like R. W. to give him a little tour of the surrounding area, but it was also seven o'clock and getting dark, and I hoped they wouldn't stay up too long. I remarked to Jackie Marshall, "I hope he comes back while there's still plenty of light to land."

Jackie didn't say anything. He just studied the sky as the plane flew out of view. "I wish they'd come on back," I muttered, feeling parental. "I don't like them staying up so long."

Thousands watched with us as the sound of the plane engines returned in about fifteen minutes. R. W. brought the Beechcraft in from the opposite direction, not unusual because he let the wind determine which angle he landed from. He would have to clear a small hill and set down quickly because the strip was so short.

The plane cleared the hill and descended toward the strip, landing lights on and gear down. "He's going to have to get down fast or he won't have time to stop," I said idly. Then I saw the landing gear fold up and heard the engine power increase. Apparently R. W. had figured it the same way I had and was going to make another run at it.

The second time it was clear he was having the same problem, and now I was worried. "Too fast!" I said. "He'll never get it down."

But I had seen him do it before. R. W. would quickly cut power, causing the plane to dip toward the ground and bounce, hoping it would stay on the ground. And now he did just that. "I hope it doesn't bounce too much," I said, but it bounced high.

The plane was still traveling too fast, and if it came down again, he would never be able to stop on the runway. Before the plane dipped again, I heard R. W. throttle up and the plane lifted. But it was soon pointed straight up! Even a novice like me knew that was no good. "Oh, no," I prayed. "Please, no."

The engines shrieked and I started running onto the strip, followed by many others. The big, ungainly plane, no longer aerodynamic, sputtered and stalled. As if in slow motion it stopped its straight climb, turned over, and plunged toward the ground.

I was on a dead run as the Beechcraft slammed to the strip and burst into flames. Within seconds I could feel the heat searing my face. The cabin door had been blown off by the impact. I fought sobs in my throat and hoped against hope that the three had been thrown clear.

The canopy had been shattered and I could see R. W. through the cockpit, still strapped in, not moving. I couldn't see Bill! I had to get to them.

Just as I started into the flames someone grabbed me and pulled me off the ground. I fought and kicked with all my might, screaming, "Let me go! Let me go! I've got to get to them!"

I didn't know it was Jake Hess who had kept me from certain death, or that I had kicked bruises all over his legs and shins. He could see there was no hope for anyone still on that plane. And all three were still there. Hysterical, I was dragged to the hangar as I watched emergency personnel extinguish the fire and then carefully extract three bodies from that charred, smoldering skeleton of the plane. They were burned beyond recognition, but it was some small comfort to learn later that the impact had broken their necks and they would have been dead before they burned.

I stood stunned near the hangar where we were to sing. *It can't be,* was all I could think. *I'll wake up and it'll be over.*

But it was true.[3]

Cecil had been visiting his wife and new son in the hospital again that night in Memphis. He was sitting on the edge of the bed, holding Doris's hand when she took a phone call. Cecil could tell something was terribly wrong. "It can't be," she said over and over. "It just can't be."

She hung up and stared blankly at Cecil, tears filling her eyes. "They've been killed," she said. "R. W. and Bill in a plane crash. They're both dead."

Cecil thought she had misunderstood and immediately left for his father Roy's home. "Daddy was in the street crying when I got there," Cecil said. "That's when I knew for sure."

Back to James's account:

All I wanted to do was to get to a phone and talk to my people in Memphis. But by the time I called, everyone had heard and was worried about me. Jake Hess put his arm around me and spoke gently. "Come on, James. Let us take you home."

We rode silently in the Statesmen's big automobile through the dark night, and my heart was dark too. "I'll never sing again," I kept telling myself. "I'll never sing another note as long as I live. I'm through."

The Blackwood Brothers at Memphis Municipal Airport with their twin Beechcraft. It was in this plane that R.W. and Bill lost their lives.

Late that night we arrived in Memphis and I was delivered to Doyle's house, where everyone was gathered. Jake and Big Chief took me to the door, each with a hand under one arm. They virtually carried me inside, and when they let go I sank to the floor, sobbing.

Our pastor, James Hamill of the First Assembly of God in Memphis, was there with the family. He had had to break the news to the wives.[4]

Indeed, as the Statesmen had been speeding James back to Memphis in the night, Pastor Hamill and his wife had rushed to Bill Lyles' home. Ruth greeted them warmly, her hands covered in bread dough. But she soon put two and two together and realized there would be no reason, except bad news, for them to be dropping in on her on a Wednesday night, especially with such somber looks.

Then it was on to R. W.'s home, where his sons Ron and Winston were just young boys. Ron says, "I remember that day well. I had a premonition, and I think God was preparing me. During the day I remember looking at the sky and thinking, *Something's gonna happen to Dad*. When Pastor Hamill showed up at our house, before he could tell me, I knew. Mother was on the phone. She had heard from someone that there had been an accident, and she was trying to locate Dad. She was crying, because she couldn't reach him, and then the pastor was there and everything erupted."

Winston, a few years younger, recalls Pastor Hamill saying, "Your daddy won't be coming home no more. Something's happened."

Jim Hamill, original lead singer of the Kingsmen Quartet in the late 1950s, with evangelist and author David Ring who inspired us with his story of preaching despite his affliction of cerebral palsy.

The great James Blackwood singing with son Jimmy.

"It's just as real today as it was then," Winston says. "We were just talking about it the other day, and tears came up in my eyes."

James:

After tearfully trying to recount what I had seen, I was put to bed and fell into an exhausted sleep. When I awoke at 6 A.M., the radio was playing a tribute to R. W. and Bill. I was barely able to bear it. All the news broadcasts carried the story. Arthur Godfrey told his audience. Walter Winchell included it in his report. Still I couldn't believe it. It was as if I was unable to make it compute in my mind. How could it be?[5]

On Friday, July 2, 1954, the funeral for R. W. Blackwood and Bill Lyles was held in the Ellis Municipal Auditorium in Memphis. Hovie Lister and the Statesmen handled the arrangements, including having several singing groups (including the Speer Family) join as a choir to sing "Does Jesus Care?" and "Known Only to Him." The governor of the state, the head of the Southern Baptist Convention, and Bill and R. W.'s own pastor officiated.

James was convinced he would never sing again, but after a heart-to-heart talk with his pastor, he somehow stumbled back out on tour and tried to fill the commitments he had made from July 4 through July 15. He remembers little from that period, can't imagine singing, and has vague memories of mixing and matching duets and trios, and even of Big Chief Wetherington of the Statesmen filling in occasionally.

The group had scheduled a break beginning July 15, which gave James time to decide what he was going to do. Roy and Doyle were running the music and record sales side of the business, and neither was interested in coming back to the stage. Cecil was available, but he was nineeen years old and a brand-new father. He had little experience except with his own little local group, which had had the remarkable foresight of rejecting a young truck driver named Elvis Presley. They thought he would be limited to only lead singing because he didn't seem to know how to blend well. Finally James asked Cecil to join the group.

Cecil accepted, but not eagerly. He recalls: "R. W. was thirteen years older than I was, and I didn't get to see him much because the group traveled so much, but he had been my hero. I was devastated at his death.

"Coming into the group as a nineteen-year-old was so heavy that I had nervous problems for a while. I was flattered to be asked, but I knew as well as everyone else did that I was no replacement at baritone for R. W.

"Everyone thought I was so timid and so bashful, but really I just felt inadequate taking my brother's place. I tried to sing and sound like him, but I was the baby of the group, so it was a big challenge."

The next problem was replacing Bill Lyles, as if that was possible. James says he didn't want to replace him for a while, but every time he prayed about it, J. D. Sum-

ner came to mind. That was ironic, because the six-foot-five-inch Sumner, with clearly the lowest voice of any professional singer, was doing well with one of the other top groups, the Sunshine Boys. The Sunshine Boys and the Blackwood Brothers had never gotten along. In fact, J. D. had heard that the Blackwoods had said something derogatory about his group, even to the point of questioning their salvation. To settle things, and apparently to prove how saved and sanctified he was, J. D. and Ace Richman of the Sunshine Boys vowed to whip R. W. and James the next time they saw them.

Now, as James continued to audition other basses and ask around, everyone seemed to mention J. D. Jake Hess assured him J. D. was the only man who could handle the job.

J. D. recalls:

I was at my home in Atlanta and we had just got through eating supper when the news come on. They said the Blackwood Brothers had had a plane crash in Clanton, Alabama, that killed R. W. and Bill Lyles. I'm sitting there in just my pants with no shirt on. Something told me and I knew just as well as I was sitting in that chair that I was going to replace Bill and become the bass singer in the Blackwood Brothers. I knew it.

Funny thing was, we didn't like one another. During those days, competition was a lot different than it is now. About six months before, R. W. had made a statement that the Sunshine Boys were infidels. Well, hey, I was raised in the same church that the Blackwoods was.

I'm sure R. W. didn't mean nothing by it. He just was trying to cut us. It was just his way of getting at someone. I sent James word that I was going to whip him. And Ace

The Masters V Quartet (from l): Hovie Lister, Jake Hess, James Blackwood, J.D. Sumner, Rosie Rozell.

Richman of the Sunshine Boys, who was much bigger than I am, said he was going to whip R. W.

Well, we finally played a benefit in Birmingham for Bobby Strickland's wife when he got killed, and we was there with the Blackwoods. Before the show R. W. came to us. He said, "I understand that you all wanted to whip us. We don't want to fight, but I'm not here to talk you out of it if nothing else will do you. But," he said, "I will be man enough to apologize for the things I've said. I had no business saying 'em, and I apologize for having implied that you all were atheists. I know better than that."

We shook hands and that was that. I always thought that was pretty big of R. W. to do that, but I can't say we and the Blackwoods were buddies after that. When James called me to join them, I really meant to turn him down. James told me he'd done a lot of praying about it. And I'd done a lot of praying about it. And quartets back in them days, we were immature and stupid to an extent. That's why I say that youth sometimes is a bad thing when it comes to having good sense.

When I started to leave to go tell James no, Ace Richman told me, "George (they all called me George, just for fun), I've been with the Sunshine Boys six years, and I love you. But you go on now and take that job, and you tell them they got the best bass singer in the world. You go ahead and take it, because it's a better job."

James offered me my choice of a salary of $14,000—$10,000 plus commission—or part ownership of the quartet. I figured if he could afford a salary like that, I'd do even better as a part owner. In the long run, it proved to be the thing to do. I've just always been at the right place at the right time. And I believe it's been under God's direction. In fact, I know it.

James and J. D. would become fast friends. James told me, "J. D. and I spent more years together than we've spent with our wives—twelve years with the Blackwood Brothers, eight years with the Masters V." They were connected as business partners and friends. J. D. adds, "We were always together—our families were like kinfolk."

Back to James's account:

So there we were, reorganized but still shattered and unsure. We were not the same group we had been. We had reached the pinnacle and plunged back, like the Beechcraft. Now we had to rebuild and believe that God would still use us for His glory.

Our first appearance with the new personnel—Jackie at the piano, me on lead, Bill Shaw as tenor, Cecil at baritone, and J. D. as the bass—was one of the toughest performances I have ever tried to make. It came on my thirty-fifth birthday, August 4, 1954, in the airport hangar at Clanton, within sight of the scorched spot where R. W. and Bill Lyles had crashed. Johnny Ogburn's father had organized the memorial concert to the three victims as a way of showing that the Peach Festival would be back and that life goes on.

I was still reeling and can hardly believe some of the publicity photos of that time that show me smiling. I did the whole concert with tightly clenched fists, nearly introducing Cecil as R. W. and J. D. as Bill.

I was in a state of shock for several days, and when the shock wore off the grief came on strong. There were days when I wondered if I had made the right decision to go on. We were back on the road in a seven-passenger car. Hard as it was to sleep at all, I began having nightmares. I imagined Bill and R. W. back in the group as if nothing had happened. I gave a double take and the group members became Cecil and J. D. again.

Then I would dream I was onstage with the new boys and see R. W. and Bill come into the back of an auditorium, smiling and waving at us. Somehow they had escaped the fiery crash and were still alive, and they were headed up to join us. Then I would wake up crying.

I couldn't stand it after a while, when the dreams kept coming and coming. I prayed and asked the Lord to deliver me from that torment. One night I dozed off, choked up about how close my close-as-a-brother nephew R. W. was to my own father, who had been in heaven since 1951. That night I dreamed I saw clear as day R. W. arriving in heaven and rushing into Daddy's arms. I was so happy I cried tears of joy, and when I woke I felt it had been of God. It was as if I had really been given a glimpse of their joyous reunion, and I never again had a haunting dream about R. W. and Bill's return.[6]

It was as if everything came full circle for James and the Blackwood Brothers when the new group was invited again to appear on *Arthur Godfrey's Talent Scouts* program in 1956. Again they won, and again it was one of the noisiest things that had happened in gospel music.

The Blackwoods would forever be marked by the tragedy that had struck them at mid-century. As personnel changed, James always put together interesting combinations, including groups that made use of his own son Jimmy. Through changing personnel and the shifting tastes of audiences, any group that used the Blackwood name and had James involved captured the fancy of a large section of the populace.

James pulled away from full-time quartet singing in 1981 but got back in when the Masters V was organized. He and J. D. of the old Blackwoods joined Jake Hess, Hovie Lister, and Rosie Rozell of the old Statesmen and enjoyed eight years of grueling travel as an all-star gospel quartet of legends.

He remains one of the most beloved pioneers and models of integrity to the many young people who would like to follow in his footsteps. There are days when I feel closer to James's age than I do to the newcomers who bring back so many memories of my own hopeful beginning in this industry. But that's when I realize James was a model and a mentor then and remains one now.

Looking at James Blackwood, we who have enjoyed the journey and endured the valleys should pray that we will finish well, as he is doing.

The 1951 Statesmen with Hovie Lister at the piano, Jake Hess, Cat Freeman (Vestal Goodman's brother), Doy Ott, and Big Chief Wetherington.

Seven

Another Living Legend

In any field, there's always a standard by which all other art is measured. In the Southern gospel quartet field, most agree the standard would have to be Hovie Lister and the sensational Statesmen. Organized in 1948 in Atlanta, Georgia, the Statesmen established a level of excellence difficult for other quartets to achieve for years to come. A bona fide original in any field is hard to find, but the Statesmen were truly originals in every sense of the word.

They were inventive and disciplined and always in relentless pursuit of perfection in their harmonies, their stage performance, and their recording. They consistently displayed a level of professionalism equaled by few in their field at that time but the Blackwoods. Jerry Crutchfield, one of today's well-known producers but a young, aspiring quartet hopeful back in the 1950s, remembers a friend saying in 1951, "Jerry, I heard a new group last night in Jackson, Tennessee, and trust me, life is never going to be the same again in our field."

The first appearance of the Statesmen was a shot heard round the gospel world.

Setting a goal and persevering toward it are important in any field. The apostle Paul wrote, "I press toward the mark for the prize of the high calling of God in Christ

The original Statesmen Quartet on the stage of the Grand Ole Opry (from l): Bobby Strickland, Jake Hess, Bervin Kendrick, Big Chief Wetherington, and Hovie Lister.

Jesus." These young men of song set a goal and pursued it with unprecedented energy.

Their day usually started with a live, 6:30 A.M. radio show in Atlanta, after which they would walk as a group eight blocks to a local cafeteria for breakfast. They'd be back at the radio station at 8:30 to rehearse until their 12:30 live show. Then they'd depart for an evening concert somewhere within driving distance of Atlanta.

Few other groups practiced as much as the Statesmen. Many quartets developed a sound and a repertoire and sang the same stuff everywhere they went. They might be good and exciting, but eventually, they would grow stale. And when personnel changed, the learning curve would hurt them, especially if they weren't used to working hard all the time. The legendary Jake Hess left more than one group when he grew frustrated at their lack of willingness to rehearse.

When a quartet has great voices and a good pianist, they're going to sound better than what most people hear locally, even if they don't rehearse constantly. But when groups work at their crafts, the way James Blackwood and Hovie Lister pushed the Blackwood Brothers and the Statesmen, the resulting sound is far better than even their stiffest competition.

The personnel of the Statesmen would change several times over the years, but Hovie was the constant. He had formed the group as a very young man, and he always looked for talent and attitude. The one quality that marked any Statesman was a willingness to work and work hard.

No matter how exhausting the schedule, the audience never seemed to detect any fatigue when it was time for the Statesmen to hit the stage. They were energy personified, and they sang with a joy so contagious it would electrify any audience. They simply enjoyed what they did. As Jake says of his years with the group, "That bunch just loved to sing. They were the singingest bunch you've ever been around. And whether we were working that night or not, we were just together singing all the time. And singing as much as we did, I guess we just developed our own style. To my knowledge, we didn't pattern ourselves after anybody."

In 1947, at age 21, Hovie Lister hosted what he called the world's first gospel DJ show on WCON, sponsored by the Adams Motor Company.

One of the first gospel quartets I heard on the radio was the Statesmen. And though they weren't on the first Wally Fowler All-Night Singing at the Ryman in Nashville in 1948, they were there in 1949 when I was there, and they just about took over the audience. J. D. Sumner always said that the only way to out-sing the Statesmen was to get up earlier in the morning than they did.

Hovie Lister and the Statesmen have always been headquartered in Atlanta, but Hovie was born in Greenville, South Carolina, on September 17, 1926. His father's father was a teacher in the singing schools and his mother's father was a Baptist preacher. Hovie was

raised in the Baptist church, surrounded by music and preaching. He began piano lessons when he was six and remembers that his father sat in on both his weekly lesson and his two-hour-a-day practice sessions, which continued for ten years.

You'd think two hours a day would be grueling for a little boy, and it's true Hovie missed out on some of the normal joys of childhood. But he loved music and the piano, and he really loved the response he received when he would show off his talent to friends, relatives, church members, and strangers. A little boy who practiced that much became a natural, and the more ani-mated he was at the piano, the more people seemed to love it.

From his earliest days, people remember that little Hovie played with abandon, eyes wide, mouth open in a huge grin, playing to the crowd all the way. By ten he was playing in church, having to turn sideways and stretch to reach the pedals. At fourteen he accompanied the Lister Brothers Quartet, made up of his father and uncles. A man in his church took him to the county jail every Sunday morning to play at a service there. And when the famed evangelist Mordecai Ham (who was preaching when a young Billy Graham made his salvation decision) came to town, fourteen-year-old Hovie was tabbed to play for his services.

Ham was so impressed that he took Hovie with him for the rest of the summer to his revivals in that region. It proved an invaluable experience for the young man, sitting under evangelistic preaching, seeing people come to Christ, and being exposed to people throughout the South.

Later that same year, just before he turned fifteen, Hovie persuaded his father to let him try to sell the local radio station on a live program for the Lister Brothers Quartet. Hovie boldly told the station manager that he would personally sell advertising for the program, which was all the man needed to hear. The quartet was invited in for an audition and passed. Hovie's father and uncles were astounded. Because of Hovie, they were on the air every week.

Hovie didn't know that his father had been salting away a little money every week so that he could send his son off to a summer session of the Stamps-Baxter

Hovie Lister selling Saltine crackers, 1953. Nabisco was their television sponsor.

School of Music in Dallas. The summer before his senior year in high school, the sixteen-year-old accepted the gift from his proud father and set off alone on the train to Dallas. After six weeks of intensive training, Hovie impressed Stamps-Baxter enough that they asked him to fill in for two weeks for a vacationing pianist in one of their quartets, the Lone Stars, in Raleigh, North Carolina.

The two weeks turned into the rest of the summer for Hovie when the group realized he could sing. After filling in for the pianist, he filled in for the tenor, then the baritone, and then the lead singer as all squeezed in their vacations, taking advantage of the versatile utility man.

The experience proved invaluable for Hovie. It settled in his young mind that there was nothing else he wanted to do but play the piano for a quartet and maybe, one day, have his own group. After high school he played for a part-time quartet in Chattanooga, Tennessee, and supplemented his income by teaching piano in the Stamps-Baxter office there.

Over the next few years Hovie would sign on and play for the famous LeFevre Trio, the Homeland Harmony Quartet (for twenty dollars a week), and the Rangers Quartet. All these groups were headquartered in Atlanta, along with groups like the Harmoneers and the Sunshine Boys.

Not long after Hovie joined the Rangers, they moved to Charlotte, but he wasn't happy there. After about a year he returned to Atlanta and rejoined the LeFevres. He was barely twenty-one years old when he added to his résumé hosting a gospel radio show in Decatur, Georgia. He may have been the first-ever gospel deejay.

Out of high school only a few years, Hovie had already worked with several gospel singing legends. Besides the LeFevres, he had been in groups with the great Bobby Strickland, Connor Hall, Big Jim Waites, Denver Crumpler, and many more. "All the while I was doing this," he says, "I was thinking that if I just got a few more years' experience, I could start my own group. That became my dream."

Hovie's enthusiasm almost got ahead of his ability to pull it off. He had become friends with the son of the chairman of the board of the *Atlanta Constitution* and talked his way into a meeting with the man. The *Constitution* was about to put a new radio station on the air, to compete with the *Atlanta Journal*, which operated the famous WSB (home of the Grand Ole Opry).

Hovie sat in the office of the powerful chairman in the *Constitution*'s new building in Atlanta, trying to convince the man that he needed a gospel quartet on at six in the morning to catch the farmers and the factory workers. The chairman was impressed and almost immediately gave Hovie the time slot. The only problem was, Hovie didn't have a group. He was playing temporarily for the LeFevres. But this was the opportunity of a lifetime.

Hovie knew from his experience with other groups that radio was the key to exposure and for arranging what he called "your 'be ats.' That way you could arrange your schedule and tell people where you were going to 'be at.'" As a rule, quartets were not paid to sing on the radio. They traded their talent for that exposure and the ability to build a concert base.

The chairman of the *Constitution* asked, "How will you boys eat?"

Hovie tried to tell him what the usual arrangement was, and that they hoped to start building an income with engagements.

"Well, how about we pay you boys fifty dollars a week each?"

Hovie was nearly overcome, but now he knew he had to come clean. He admitted he really didn't have the quartet yet. He offered to play records until he rounded up personnel, and he was relieved when the chairman hesitantly agreed. Interestingly, Hovie's morning show was followed by one hosted by a local comedian named Dick Van Dyke.

Hovie worried that as a twenty-one-year-old, he didn't have the stature to attract the big names he really wanted. He was younger than every one of them. And yet he was a perfectionist even then. He decided he would go after the best of the best and put together an all-star list of men who were not only talented but also dedicated to the Lord and to excellence. He started with Mosie Lister, who would be with the group only a short while. Mosie didn't like traveling, and he felt called to write music. He became one of the most prolific and beloved gospel songwriters ever.

Only true fans and historians remember that Mosie Lister was a member of the original Statesmen. And very few people know that Mosie and Hovie, despite their strikingly similar first names and identical last names, are not related. They met when Hovie was playing for the Rangers and Mosie was with the Melody Masters.

Hovie was able to get Bobby Strickland as his tenor, Bervin Kendrick as baritone, and Gordon Hill as bass. With Mosie on lead, he had his group. What he didn't have was a name, and even that was crucially important to the young entrepreneur. From the beginning he wanted a group that was a cut above with a name that would do the idea justice.

His first thought was to call his quartet the Senators, but the more he thought about it, the more he leaned toward something even more impressive.

"What I had in my young mind was that I wanted a group that was outstanding, something that was going to be tops from the very git-go," Hovie explained. "This group has got to be something that's tried and proven. You don't get to be a Statesman until you have proven that you've got what it takes. People call you 'senator' if you've been elected, but they only call you a states-man if you've earned it with your reputation. I wanted the Statesmen to be a group singers aspired to, not where they started their careers."

All his young life, Hovie was interested in politics. The Georgia governor at that time was Herman Talmadge. His father before him had been elected governor three times, and Hovie had helped out in one of the campaigns. "So the governor knew me somewhat. I recalled that he published a monthly newsletter called *The Statesman*. And I went to him and asked him if he would mind if I used that name for my quartet. He said he'd be honored."

Governor Talmadge also offered to name the Statesmen "ambassadors of good will for the state of Georgia." Hovie and his quartet used that tag for decades.

From the first, the young Hovie Lister was a leader, even though everybody in the group was older than he was. He was a pusher, insistent that each member devote himself to the Lord and to the music. Everything was intended to contribute to the product, and the product was blessing the people and praising the Lord. That's why Hovie considered the quartet full-time work. They sang on the radio together, ate together, rehearsed together, traveled together, and performed concerts together. There was no "down" time. It seemed every spare minute went into rehearsing.

Hovie's view was that anybody could get a group of singers together, and if they were lucky enough to have some talent, they could have fun and impress people. But Hovie was obsessed with being the best. He regularly checked out the competition.

But the day would come when he realized that if you couldn't beat the Blackwoods, you could join them.

The Statesmen Quartet (from l): Rosie Rozell, Jake Hess, Hovie Lister, Big Chief Wetherington, Doy Ott.

The Statesmen and the Blackwood Brothers sang two separate styles and were two very different groups. Hovie's approach was loud, fast, swingy, and pop. He cared every bit as much about diction and enunciation and being understood as the classy Blackwoods, but he would also do whatever it took to get the loudest applause, the biggest laugh—whatever. The Statesmen dressed the flashiest, had the most complex arrangements, the tightest harmonies, and were all around the most exciting group on any stage. They were simply more animated than anyone else, and their music was right there at the top too.

As competitive as the Blackwoods and the Statesmen were through the years, they had great respect for each other and worked together for a long, long time. Hovie and James were like two peas in a pod, though Hovie was more of a jumping bean.

Personnel changes were the norm for the Statesmen, right from the beginning, and through the years fans have compared and contrasted the various combinations.

The Statesmen out West (from l): Hovie Lister, Rosie Rozell, Jake Hess, Big Chief Wetherington, Doy Ott.

The first sound, with Mosie Lister on lead, was very smooth and tight. Aycel Soward, who had sung with the LeFevres, replaced Gordon Hill as bass, and Mosie wanted off the road within the first year. He felt called to write and arrange, and the industry is the better for it. Not that Mosie wasn't a good singer. He was. But he's nearly unmatched as a composer.

Hovie recalls, "When Mosie said he wanted to drop out, I said, 'I don't have anybody to take your place.' Mosie said, 'What about Jake Hess?' I said, 'Jake Hess? He sings like a girl. I don't want him.'" But a few days later, in a conversation with his own father, Hovie mentioned his need for a good lead singer. "Jake Hess is your man," his father said, and the rest is history.

Hovie didn't know Jake well. But he'd heard enough about him to try him out. In truth, Hovie was undecided about Jake and considered replacing him for a long time after he joined the group. But Jake worked hard to increase his power, took voice lessons, and eventually won Hovie's approval.

While with the Sunny South Quartet, Jake had sung with a wonderful bass singer of Cherokee descent named James Wetherington. When it turned out that the slightly older and very talented Soward agreed with Hovie that he wasn't quite the showman the Statesmen needed, Wetherington was brought in as the new bass. Hovie introduced him one night as the Big Chief, due to his Indian heritage, and that was the way Wetherington was known for the next quarter century.

Over the years, the Statesmen would have many outstanding tenors, beginning with Bobby Strickland. The first time I heard the Statesmen on a Capitol record, the group was made up of Bobby as tenor, Bervin Kendrick as baritone, Jake Hess the lead, and the Big Chief as bass.

Bobby Strickland was a jolly, friendly young man, and one of those great tenors of his time. He would later leave the group to start the Crusaders Quartet and to prepare for a preaching ministry, but his career was cut short when he was killed in a car accident at the age of thirty-three.

One of Bobby's biggest contributions to the Statesmen was to recommend his good friend Bervin Kendrick as the first baritone. Bervin had a smooth voice that added to a special blend.

But the unique sound of this group was eventually molded around the fresh new voice of lead singer Jake Hess, who was perhaps the first crooner and real stylist of the gospel music field. He was not only a great singer, but also a true Christian gentleman with an engaging smile. He used his eyes, his lips, his smile, his gestures—everything—to communicate every syllable.

Jake became the model for many an aspiring lead singer. Kids across the country began mimicking his vocal stylings and gestures in hopes that one day they might become the next Jake Hess.

Hovie kept Mosie on retainer for new compositions and arrangements, recognizing his special talent. And Jake's voice was the perfect match for Mosie's work. Mosie says, "When they started asking me for material, I was ready to start writing some complicated stuff. They wanted it innovative. They wanted it new, different, fresh, loud, and boisterous. It was fun."

Some of that modern harmony got the Statesmen into trouble in the early days. Some of the conservative Christian radio stations actually made a point of breaking Statesmen records on the air. There was just too much tempo in some of those early tunes, and no one could imagine that God was pleased with that!

Jake Hess recalls, "With some of Mosie's arrangements—with all those modern chords—people in the singing convention resented that. They said, 'Hey, that group sings la's instead of sol's! You just can't do that in Christian music!'"

I work with a lot of contemporary artists and, from time to time, one of them will come to me and complain about being criticized. I enjoy telling them that this is nothing new. Nearly fifty years ago a young group called the Statesmen suffered their share of criticism.

The next tenor to join the Statesmen was Cat Freeman, Vestal Goodman's brother. As the eldest brother in that musical family, he had been to every music school available and had taught his sisters to sing. He was a clown and a cutup, but his distinctly high voice added a special touch to the Statesmen's sound.

Hovie enlisted in military service in 1950 during the Korean conflict, and veteran musician and keyboard man Doy Ott stepped in during that time. He stayed with the quartet as baritone when Hovie returned, and many think he was the smoothest voice they ever had. Hovie was grateful for Doy's versatility as an arranger, parts coach, and pianist. Besides singing a beautiful part, he could lead a rehearsal in Hovie's absence and was even known to take over for Hovie on the piano in the middle of a song on the radio without anyone being the wiser.

That particular group of Statesmen was the one Jake was referring to when he said they were the singingest bunch he'd ever been around. They would sing to kill time if they showed up early for an engagement. They would load the car when it was over, and if Hovie hadn't finished settling up with the promoter, they would gather around the piano and sing some more. It wasn't just a job to them, and they seemed never to grow tired of it. They had a desire to sing.

Jake was such a long-standing member of the Statesmen that he became identified with them forever.

When the group evolved in 1953 to where Denver Crumpler sang tenor, Doy Ott baritone, and Jake and Chief the lead and bass, many consider that the best personnel the group ever had. In fact many, many experts, Ben and Brock Speer among them, believe that was the perfect quartet, the best that ever sang together.

Hovie had wanted to add the talented Crumpler for years. Denver had spent sixteen years with the Rangers Quartet. They had been widely considered the best in the field until a tragic auto accident depleted their ranks. Meanwhile the Blackwoods were coming on strong, and then the Statesmen began. Hovie had wanted Denver Crumpler from the beginning, and now he had finally gotten him.

Crumpler had such a high, clear, unstrained tenor voice that Hovie didn't mind criticism that sometimes it seemed to dominate rather than blend. "If a voice is gonna stick out," Hovie said about Crumpler's tenor, "that's the kind of a voice you wanna hear!"

Jake Hess was so excited about Denver joining the group that he could hardly wait to perform with him. "He was the epitome of a pro," Jake said. Jake also remembers that Denver had a fantastic work ethic and was always ready to perform from the first number. "Some tenors would ask the quartet manager to not feature them until they loosened up by the fourth or fifth tune. Not Crump. He was ready from the git-go."

The Statesmen recorded for RCA Victor, had their own Nabisco television show, and quickly became the toast of gospel music. Most said only the Blackwoods even held a candle to them. The best of the family groups were the Speer Family and the LeFevres, but of all the all-male quartets, it seemed everyone was either just hoping or pretending to be as good as the Statesmen and the Blackwoods.

When those two groups agreed to cooperate, to double book and work together about three-fourths of the time, it was a stroke of genius. Each group had its own following, a distinct crowd. But when they got together on purpose, audiences went wild.

There was also a lot of talk about which was best, who was favored, who had the best bass, the best lead, the best tenor, the best piano man. It's all a matter of opinion, of course, but the controversy and friendly rivalry brought out the best in each group.

It was not as it had been in the early days when groups pulled each other's power cord or constantly tried to upstage one another. Now, what was good for one group was good for the other, and they encouraged each other. Both groups admit that "competing" with the other for the audience's approval nearly every night made them work harder, rehearse longer, look for better songs, and strive for more complex and pleasing arrangements. The Blackwoods got classier. The Statesmen got more exciting. The fans of gospel music were the winners.

When the Blackwoods won the *Arthur Godfrey Talent Scouts* program in June 1954 and the two groups planned to appear together at the Chilton County Peach Festival in Clanton, Alabama, both quar-

The late, great Rosie Rozell, tenor of the legendary Statesmen Quartet.

tets were at their absolute peak of personnel. A poster advertising the event shows the Blackwood Brothers with James, Jackie Marshall, Bill Shaw, Bill Lyles, and

Jack Toney replaced Jake Hess in the Statesmen Quartet.

R. W. The Statesmen pictured were Hovie, Jake, Doy Ott, Denver Crumpler, and the Big Chief.

The tragedy that struck on that last day in June 1954 robbed the music world of one of the greatest acts imaginable—the Blackwoods-Statesmen. With a single punch, the plane crash that day left the Blackwoods decimated.

The Statesmen went on to win the *Arthur Godfrey Talent Scout* show themselves, but they suffered their own tragedy in 1957. Denver Crumpler died suddenly of a heart attack at age forty-four, and a major element of their sound, not to mention their tight-knit family, was suddenly gone.

Cat Freeman was brought back to take Crumpler's place. Cat, who died in 1989, is remembered as one of the smoothest tenors ever in the gospel music field. His style enabled the group to do very sophisticated and difficult close harmonies.

"Cat was a very strong tenor," Hovie says. "And he was one of the funniest and easiest guys to get along with."

Another young man brought a special energy and excitement to the tenor part for Hovie and the Statesmen. Rosie Rozell was from Oklahoma and had attracted the notice of the Statesmen when they had toured there and heard him sing with a group called the Tulsa Trumpeteers. He was different from all the other tenors the Statesmen had employed and brought a certain amount of emotion and soul that none of the others had offered. His beautiful rendition of "O What a Savior" is a gospel classic.

O What a Savior

Once I was straying in sin's dark valley;
No hope within could I see,
They searched thru heaven and found a Savior
To save a poor lost soul like me.

He left the Father with all His riches,
With calmness sweet and serene;
Came down from heaven and gave His lifeblood
To make the vilest sinner clean.

Death's chilly waters I'll soon be crossing;
His hand will lead me safe o'er.
I'll join the chorus in that great City,
And sing up there forevermore.

O what a Savior! O hallelujah!
His heart was broken on Calvary.
His hands were nail-scarred; His side was riven.
He gave His lifeblood for even me.[1]

Hovie mists up as he recalls the very first time the Statesmen sang "O What a Savior." He wanted to feature his new tenor, and Rosie had worked and worked on that beautiful, haunting, soulful piece. Before a big crowd in Detroit, Hovie introduced Rosie and the song. "I felt God gave me an unusually anointed introduction for it," Hovie recalls, "though I don't recall all I said. I know I didn't suggest any response, so what happened was totally of the Lord."

Rosie began to sing, and about halfway through, Hovie says, "I see people getting up out of their seats and coming toward the front. As they got closer I could see they were weeping. As soon as we finished that song I grabbed the microphone and said, 'If you will all come backstage, I'll meet with you and pray with you right now.' A number of people were saved that night. That was a spontaneous outpouring of the Spirit of the Lord. It was thrilling."

Rosie would sing with the Statesmen until 1970 and again for a time in 1973. After singing with his own group for a few years, Rosie became a church musician until 1981 when he would join Jake Hess, Hovie Lister, J. D. Sumner, and James Blackwood as a member of the Masters V. Health problems forced him from the road in the early 1980s. He died in February 1995.

One of the all-time great Statesmen songs, trademarked by Jake's lead rendition, was a Mosie Lister tune called "Where No One Stands Alone." It happened to be a favorite of Elvis Presley, and occasionally he would show up at a Statesmen show in Memphis and request it. He later recorded it, singing the Statesmen arrangement, and made it a hit.

Hovie remembers that one night during a concert in Memphis in the late 1950s, "we were singing and Elvis came in with a few of his bodyguards, and I could see him standing offstage. He kept trying to get my attention and mouth, 'Where No One Stands Alone.' I kept shaking him off and he kept on saying it, but I just ignored him so we could get to our finale.

"When we finally finished and we bowed to the crowd I thought, *Man, this is the loudest ovation we've ever gotten!* Then I felt a tap on my shoulder, and it was Elvis. He said to Jake, 'Leave the stage. We're singin' "Where No One Stands Alone," and I've got the lead.'"

Jake says, "Elvis knew Mosie's songs better than I did."

Where No One Stands Alone

Once I stood in the night with my head bowed low,
In the darkness as black as could be;
And my heart felt alone and I cried,
"O Lord, don't hide your face from me."

Like a king I may live in a palace so tall,
With great riches to call my own;
But I don't know a thing in this whole wide world
That's worse than being alone.

The Golden Keys (from l): Jim Hill (writer of "What a Day That Will Be")
Harold Patrick, Clarence Claxson, Pat Duncan.

Hold my hand all the way, every hour, every day,
From here to the great unknown.
Take my hand, let me stand
Where no one stands alone.[2]

Mosie Lister remembers how the writing of that song came about:

I had been to a gospel concert in Macon, Georgia, and was driving back to Atlanta by myself, not thinking about anything at all. At about midnight I started singing the whole chorus. I got to the end and realized that this was a brand-new song. I sang it again and again, and I got home and tried to see if there was anything else that could go along with it. I found nothing for about a year. Then I read the fifty-first Psalm, and that was the key. David was lamenting how bad he felt about his sin with Bathsheba and how alone he felt. I told my wife I'd be right back, went out, and I walked around the block two times. I had the two verses by the time I came back.

Jack Toney, an exciting new young lead singer, came to the Statesmen quartet in 1963 after Jake Hess had left to start a new innovative group, the Imperials.

Jack says, "It was a dream come true when I joined the Statesmen. I had grown up listening to the radio, and I sang along then, but I never thought I'd get to join them."

Jack proved to be an impressive young talent, though the road proved hard on his home life. Jack was eventually replaced by my old friend Jim Hill, composer of "What a Day That Will Be" and founder of the Golden Keys Quartet, where my brother Danny got his start. Jim says he knew he was following some greats as lead for the Statesmen and had to decide to "just be myself and not anyone else."

The end of the dominance of the Statesmen began in 1972. Hovie was the only original member still left, though Doy Ott had been a mainstay for years and Big Chief Wetherington had been with the group nearly a quarter of a century. Gospel music was changing, but the Statesmen were still exciting and dynamic and could turn on a crowd.

Everyone considered Big Chief one of the best quartet men in the business. He was always professional and hardworking, looked good, had great rhythm, and loved to put on a show. He might not be able to slide down the scale as far as J. D. Sumner, but even J. D. acknowledges that "Chief was the most professional man to ever stand onstage."

In 1972 Chief admitted to Hovie that he had begun coughing up blood. Hovie was stunned, because Jim Wetherington was one of those guys who not only was never sick, he never even seemed to feel bad. Hovie encouraged him to fly home, but Chief wanted to tough it out.

Just before a concert in Oregon, Chief asked Hovie not to say anything until the end of the show, but to then ask if a doctor could visit them backstage. Hovie was alarmed but waited until the end, as Chief had requested. The next morning Chief was diagnosed with a blood clot in his lung. He was hospitalized there and transferred to Georgia for another week in the hospital. For about a year he was able to tour without difficulty by keeping up with his blood-thinning medication.

Most thought Chief was out of danger by the time of the National Quartet Convention in Nashville in October 1973. While other members of the group flew in

Mosie Lister, widely published songwriter.

from their homes, Chief and his wife, Elizabeth, and Hovie and his wife, Ethel, rode the Statesmen's bus from Atlanta. Hovie recalls enjoying the Wetheringtons' pictures of their daughter's wedding a few months earlier.

Big Chief seemed fine. The group performed early in the week and were to sing again Thursday night. Chief's wife, Elizabeth, says he had had no problems and was enjoying a relaxing time. Late on Thursday afternoon he told her he was going to shave and get ready for the evening performance. She was napping when she heard him fall.

I was in the lobby of the same hotel when I heard Hovie paged and saw him emerge from the coffee shop. I asked him what was up and he said he didn't know. But as he headed toward the desk and the house phone, the elevator doors opened and paramedics wheeled out a body under a sheet. We were stunned to be told it was James "Big Chief" Wetherington, gone at fifty-one.

That tragedy cast a pall over the convention, of course, and many flew out for the funeral and then back for the rest of the show. The Statesmen were never the same, though with the inevitable personnel changes, there would be many more versions. In fact, I even helped Hovie form a new group after we had done the very first "Homecoming" video. The New Statesmen released an album called "Revival" in January 1992. It was an honor to have had a little to do with it.

In 1993 Hovie went to see a specialist about an unusual feeling in his throat. A lesion was detected, and on his sixty-seventh birthday, he had it removed. "The Lord healed me," he says. "Millions of people prayed for me. Later the doctor said he couldn't even find where they cut the lesion out."

But despite the healing, the next years were not an easy time for Hovie. He was weak and tired and felt he had no more to offer the music ministry. He sensed there would be no more demand for his music. On our video "Bill and Gloria Gaither Present Hovie Lister and the Sensational Statesmen," Gloria said, "Few young singers know how the truths of their lyrics will be tested in the crucibles of life. But like great songs, great men and women do not usually develop without a struggle, without a story. For some, it is the refining fire of pain or illness; for others, it is failure, the loss of someone close and dear, the separation from children or family. But for us all, life sifts out faults, and the winds of time blow them away. What is left is certain. What is left is true. What is left is the Rock of Ages."

I asked Hovie to do a solo vocal album when he had recovered, not knowing that he was going through a rough period. "I want to be honest about that time in my life," he says. "When you called me, I thought it was a joke, because I had just told God to take a flying leap. I didn't think anybody cared. I thought everybody was a hypocrite and a crook. I thought a liquor store man had more self-respect and honor than most church people.

"You wouldn't think that a guy that had been reared like I had been reared could ever get like that. But if God had not spoken to you and you had not obeyed God and I had not accepted your invitation, there's just no telling where I would be today. And that's pretty tough, but that's the truth."

I don't know who had disappointed Hovie so deeply or what might have gotten him so depressed and dis-couraged. Whatever the cause, he had reached a desolate spot with the Lord.

What I do know is that when he sang for that album a song called "I Lost It All to Find Everything," he sang it like no one else, before or since.

I Lost It All to Find Everything

I had won all I could win, there was no place I hadn't been,
But my heart was just so needy and so poor;
Then I heard Him gently say, "Lose it all and find My way,"
So, I gave up and I found it all and more.

I was frantic to survive and I was racing to arrive
And I walked on any standing in my way;
Then I watched all my schemes die and I realized that I
Could find new life because the old had died that day.

I lost it all to find everything.
I died a pauper to become a king.
When I learned how to lose,
I found how to win.
Oh, I lost it all to find everything.[3]

Jake Hess.

Eight
The One and Only

For nearly fifty years, Jake Hess has been one of the most dominant personalities in all of gospel music. To understand Jake, you first have to understand the word "spirit." You can't be around him long before you realize that this man is bigger than life. An indestructible spirit about him looks in the face of all odds and shouts a resounding "yes!" Young and old alike love to be around Jake because of his contagious spirit. There is a graciousness about him that genuinely rejoices when a brother rejoices, and sincerely weeps when a brother weeps.

Jesus said, "Love the Lord your God with all your heart and your neighbor as yourself." That seems to come almost naturally for Jake. The comments we've received most about our "Homecoming" videos always mention that the folks included seem to "really love the Lord and each other." They often add that it's "refreshing to see that kind of love," and nearly always, such a comment is sure to include Jake Hess.

No wonder he is one of the most loved people in the gospel music field today, a role model for many young aspiring artists. Ivan Parker, a great young tenor, says

Ivan Parker singing "Oh, How Much He Cares For Me."

Jake Hess was an inspiration to him "all of my life and he never even knew it. When I was twelve and thirteen years old, Jake sang several times in Washington, D.C., at Constitution Hall. He didn't know there was a teenage

boy behind the curtain storing up memories that will never leave. If it hadn't been for Jake Hess, I might have never sung gospel music."

Jake is the first to say, "I'm far from perfect." Well, I'm not trying to pin a perfect label on anyone, but when it comes to loving God and loving each other, Jake is right near the top.

He was born in Haleyville, Alabama, on Christmas Eve in 1927, the last of twelve children born to share-croppers. He knew the value of hard work, and he knew what it meant to follow a mule, acre after dusty acre, from sunup to sundown, on a hot summer day. He recalls singing to the rear end of that mule and telling himself over and over that all he wanted to do was be a quartet singer.

Jake started singing with his brothers in the early 1940s. At only sixteen years of age, he joined the famous John Daniel Quartet of Nashville. Jake first met the legendary bass singer J. D. Sumner the next year when he left Nashville for Florida to sing with the Sunny South Quartet. He and J. D. were both in their teens, and they were crazy. The craziness didn't stop as they got older. These two characters have stayed close through the years, and when they get together there are always stories from the past.

J. D. recalls that when "Jake was about seventeen and I was nineteen, we were heading back to the hotel after a concert. There was this filling station that had a pinball machine, and me and Jake wanted to play. We kept asking our manager, Horace Floyd, if we could stop and play, and he wouldn't let us. He just kept driving.

The Melody Masters, 1947, (seated from l) Alvin Tootle, Wally Varner, (standing from l) Cat Freeman, Big Chief Wetherington, Jake Hess.

"I was sitting in the middle and Jake was sitting on the right-hand side. I told Jake, 'If you just jump out, he'll have to let us play. What's he gonna do? Just jump out.' Jake looked at me. I said, 'I'll be right behind ya.' It seemed like we were goin' about forty miles an hour, and if it hadn't been a dirt road, we'd a been killed. Jake grabbed that handle and he was gone, right out the car. I said, 'Oh Jesus, help me, I didn't mean for the fool to jump.' Well, a deal was a deal, so I had to go too. Out I went. I musta rolled a quarter of a mile."

Jake says, "J. D. looked like a big telephone pole rollin' along!"

Jake later joined the Melody Masters Quartet in Lincoln, Nebraska, who gave him the chance to develop the style of singing we've all come to know and love. That quartet was way ahead of its time—young and innovative musicians who dared to try new rhythms and harmonies. It was in this group that he sang with two of the men who would later become the nucleus of the Statesmen Quartet—Cat Freeman and Big Chief Jim Wetherington.

It was also the first time that we heard a gospel singer croon a lyric. That's something I can't do justice to on paper, and if you've yet to hear Jake's sweet crooning, I recommend one of his many records or tapes. One of his trademark tunes is still a favorite of his fans:

Faith Unlocks the Door

Prayer is the key to heaven,
but faith unlocks the door,
Words are so easily spoken,
but prayer without faith is like a boat
  without an oar;
Have faith when you speak to the Master,
That's all He asks you for,
Prayer is the key to heaven,
But faith unlocks the door.[1]

It was in the fall of 1948 that Jake got the call from Hovie Lister to join the Statesmen. With that move the Jake/Hovie combination captivated audiences all over the country for the next fifteen years. They would record thirty long-play albums on RCA Victor Records. They were in demand all over the country.

Hovie says, "Jake wanted to sing—that was his first priority—sing, sing, sing. I could tell a million jokes on Jake, but he could tell a million more on me, 'cause I never made a mistake in my life without Jake right there laughin', beatin' the floor. But seriously, Jake Hess was the epitome of the greatest quarterback of any quartet that's ever been. Jake decided that if he was gonna stay in the group, he was determined to do it and do it right. When people ask me what made Jake the legend he is, I tell them it was because he asked God to give him the tools, and he used those tools to the ultimate advantage."

Though the beginning was rocky between Jake and Hovie (Hovie thought Jake sang like a girl and considered replacing him for a long time), Jake did what he had to do to make himself into the kind of a singer Hovie loved. In fact, as Jake worked and improved, Hovie began to build the entire sound of the Statesmen around him. Mosie Lister, who did much of the composing and arranging for the group, admits he had Jake in mind almost every time he sat down to write a Statesmen tune.

Jake made up for any lack of power or range (and there wasn't much lacking!) with his ability to interpret

and deliver a phrase. He was obsessed with diction, pronunciation, the understandability of every syllable. He would use inflection, mouth shape, gestures, expressions, whatever it took to communicate exactly what he thought the lyric and tune intended to say. It was clear he was the lead, and he commanded attention.

It wasn't that he was an egotist. If anything, he served the music and the audience. And while they cheered and applauded thunderously for him, he was merely grateful they had understood the message. Hovie would be banging away and mugging at the piano, bouncing all over the stool, pulling his pant legs up to reveal red socks; Denver Crumpler would be soaring over the tight harmonies with that beautiful, piercing tenor that made people shake their heads; Doy Ott was smoothly blending, smack dab in the middle of the pitch; Big Chief Wetherington would be keeping time with his body and his voice, richly rolling the bass tones

J. D. Sumner (seated) and Jake Hess in mock formality.

in there. Jake would blend with a nice melody until it was time to take over.

Then Jake would lift those hands with the long graceful fingers, open his eyes wide, look directly at the crowd, and sing clearly, crooning, as if speaking to a baby. Regardless of the text or message, attention was riveted on him and you couldn't miss a word. He wouldn't let you. It was as if he had gently grasped your collar and wouldn't let go; best of all, you didn't want him to let go. He sang as if he meant every word, and anyone who has ever known him knows that is true.

"I didn't know I was singing a different style from anybody else," Jake says, "until we were doing the Nabisco TV series and the first letter was from a lady who wanted to know why the bald-headed man 'sang with meaningless hand motions and fat eyes.' I thought, if that's what I'm doing, I'd better change it. Hovie and I looked at some film to see what I could do different, but I found I couldn't sing when I didn't do that."

What had drawn Jake to the Statesmen was Hovie Lister. The little preacher, promoter, pianist, and quartet master was a young man with ideas, vigor, and a plan. He wanted the best quartet in history, and Jake believes he eventually put it together. "Hovie could do it all," Jake says. "He sold himself and us to everyone, and he was a good businessman."

Hovie's passion for rehearsing hit Jake right where he lived. To him, there was no substitute for practicing and learning to do a thing right. Getting up at the crack of dawn for a live radio program was nothing but fine for Jake. And "nothing but fine" was, is, and always will

be his answer to any question about his well-being. It made no difference whether he was suffering chest pains or the various ailments related to diabetes. Jake was always "nothing but fine."

And every day, after the radio program and breakfast, it was back to the radio studio for more rehearsing before the live noon show, and that was all right with Jake too. On the long drives to nightly concerts, what did the Statesmen do in the car? If it was up to Jake, or Big Chief, or most any of the Statesmen, they would keep working, harmonizing, trying something new. By the time they got to that night's venue, they were ready to see how something sounded with a piano.

For whatever misgivings Hovie Lister had at first about Jake's thin and almost feminine sounding voice, Hovie was thrilled from the beginning with Jake's work ethic. He never quit trying to improve, and when he had finally learned to broaden his range and add power and color to his tone, Hovie was convinced Jake had become the best quartet man in the business.

Jake has always had a great sense of humor, even when it comes to his hair, or lack thereof. I once told him, "Sometimes that toupee leaned left and sometimes it leaned right, as if it couldn't decide whether it was Democrat or Republican."

Jake says, "It all depended on how much time I had. It got to where after a while I'd just throw it up and run under it."

The hairpiece came about when the Statesmen were singing on the Nabisco show every week. All the other guys had full heads of hair, and Jake was starting to thin

The Imperials (from l): Jake Hess, Sherrill Nielsen, Gary McSpadden, Armond Morales, Henry Slaughter.

on top. Bill Harrison, a representative of the McCann-Erickson ad agency handling the show for Nabisco, asked to see Jake after the broadcast one night.

"He was all nervous and fumbling for words," Jake recalls. He said, 'Uh, Jake, you know, uh, all these guys have a black head of hair, and they're good-lookin' guys, and I thought maybe—'

"I decided to make it easy for him. I said, 'Bill, you buy it and I'll wear it.'"

Hovie says the first night Jake wore his toupee, "he was absolutely scared to death. He didn't know what the folks would think. And being in Macon, Georgia, of all places, where everybody knew him, well, he was terribly self-conscious."

"I was afraid to take a bow and have it fall off into some lady's lap," Jake says. "I looked so scared, Hovie hadn't given me a lead song several numbers into the program. All of a sudden a guy in bib overalls stands up and hollers, 'Brother Hovie, let the kid with the wig sing one!'"

The late Elvis Presley seldom missed a chance to say that the biggest influence on him as a young man and as a young singer was Jake Hess. Elvis's wife, Priscilla, even said she had to compete with the recordings the pop king listened to every night—often Jake Hess music. Jake sang at Elvis's funeral, but he always refused to capitalize on their friendship or his association with Elvis.

Elvis frequently had the Statesmen to his Graceland home when they were in Memphis. Jake always refused to go, and once Elvis asked him why. Jake asked him if he really wanted to know. "I do," Elvis insisted.

"Elvis, to tell you the truth, I'm not interested in your real estate. I don't want a car or even one of your Taking Care of Business pins. I just want your friendship."

Elvis stared at him and clapped him on the shoulder. "You've got it, Jake," he had said.

Jake's and Hovie Lister's lifetime friendship survived even their split in 1963. With two lesser friends it might have been more of a problem when the heart and soul of the best group around decides to move out on his own. Hovie wasn't happy about it and let Jake know. It was difficult, but they made it work and today they are the best of friends. Jake has often said, "If there wasn't a Hovie Lister, nobody would have ever heard of Jake Hess."

What happened was that Jake grew restless and began dreaming of his own group. He finally made the break in 1963 and organized the Imperials, one of the first contemporary gospel music groups. He called them the Imperials because he wanted a name that sounded regal. And regal they were with an all-star lineup—Armond Morales, Sherrill Nielsen, Gary McSpadden, and Henry Slaughter at the piano.

Jake has never been afraid to experiment with new ideas, and this one was new and very innovative. He knew how to put great voices together, and these were the best of the time.

Joe Moscheo tells an interesting story about Jake's management style when he hired him as a keyboard player in 1967:

I was playing with a group called the Prophets when I came down from Knoxville to audition for Jake. He really put me through it and hired me. The first date we played after that was at the Medinah Temple in Chicago, and I didn't have a suit yet because I was brand new to the group. Jake introduced me by saying that if I did all right that night, 'we're gonna get him a suit to match ours.' I played a few songs, and everybody seemed to like them. Then a guy in the balcony yells out, 'Get the kid a suit!'

After his tenure with the Statesmen and the Imperials, Jake started experiencing some heart problems. And for all of us who have followed Jake since then, we know what an emotional roller coaster his health has been. Artists minister out of their experiences, and for Jake that has meant finding joy in the midst of so many discouraging circumstances.

The life of a gospel singer is not an easy one for nurturing a marriage and family relationships. But you can't be around Jake Hess long before you discover how much

The Imperials with Jimmy Dean in 1965 (clockwise from upper l): Jim Murray, Greg Gordon, Terry Blackwood, Joe Moscheo, and Armond Morales.

he loves and treasures his family. It's obvious his beautiful wife, Joyce, is the love of his life, and together they have managed Jake's travels with grace and faithfulness, keeping their priorities centered on the Lord, each other, and their three children—Jake Jr., Becky, and Chris.

For eight years Jake toured with his kids and a bunch of other young people in what many experts considered the low point of his professional career. It's true that no great singers came out of that group, and they may not have had anywhere near the prestige of his previous ensembles. But to Jake it was important to spend those years with his kids. And the kids remember those years as the best of their lives, even though they knew he may have been sacrificing his own reputation.

They're all grown up now with families of their own who love to come home to Papa's house. Some time ago Gloria and I spent a day in the Hess house experiencing the warmth and love that have kept them so close over the years. Joyce is a great southern cook and we enjoyed eating together in their big comfortable kitchen, listening to funny stories and family jokes. Later, we gathered around to enjoy memories from the Hess photo albums and scrapbooks.

Becky remembered when she was fourteen at a National Quartet Convention, Jake's first appearance since a massive heart attack. "I had been backstage at concerts all my life, but I

Terry Blackwood of Andrus, Blackwood and Co., son of Doyle Blackwood and nephew of James Blackwood, both original members of the Blackwood Brothers Quartet.

Jake Hess and the Imperials (from l): Armond Morales, Jim Murray, Gary McSpadden, Henry Slaughter, Jake Hess.

remember standing back there when they introduced him, and people went crazy. People were taking pictures, and I was thrilled. All I could think of was, 'My gosh, that's my daddy.'"

And during the years she traveled and sang with her dad, Becky remembers sitting next to him as he drove thousands of miles. "We talked philosophy and faith and why people did what they did and said what they said. I'll never forget that time, learning so much, having his full attention."

Chris remembers all the friends his dad had and how impressive it was when Elvis occasionally called the house. But more important than introducing his kids to Elvis, Chris says, "He introduced us to Jesus. Dad was a Christian, and he lived his faith, even at home."

Nobody can pay a man a higher tribute than that.

J. D. Sumner and the Stamps (from l): J. D. Sumner, Rick Strickland, C. J. Almgren, (seated) Ed Hill, Ed Enoch.

Nine
The Innovative Genius

Nobody comes away from having met J. D. Sumner—or even just seeing him onstage—without knowing they have been exposed to one of the most unusual personalities the gospel music scene has ever had.

J. D. is a striking, commanding physical presence. Now in the autumn of his life, his gray hair and that craggy face show the years and the miles. But he's still six-foot-five-and-a-half and hard to miss. He's in the *Guinness Book of World Records* for having sung the lowest note in history. His vocal chords are so long and his speaking voice alone is so low that you have to listen closely to make the words resonate in your ears.

J. D. takes great pride in that he is not just a low-note "growler," as so many of the well-known low-note basses have been. He doesn't claim to have been the best bass who ever lived. There are those who would vote for Big Jim Waites, Big Chief James Wetherington, Frank Stamps, and the late great Bill Lyles. London Parris, who followed J. D. with the Blackwood Brothers, was also a powerful singer J. D. admired.

J. D. Sumner.

acter. The Blackwoods, three months before their air tragedy, were not the only ones who referred to him and his cohorts in the Sunshine Boys as infidels. J. D. says if he had it all to do again, "I'd a been a better boy." But most of his mischief was youthful recklessness.

In his own autobiography he admits that his fifty-one-year marriage was a fragile thing held together by his beloved Mary Agnes. "She was the glue," he admits, and he mists up whenever he mentions her. She died in 1992.

J. D. feels that he committed himself to Christ anew, this time for good, when he lost Mary Agnes. "I was always a-comin' back to God," he says. "I was always a Christian and I meant well, but I had a lot of startin' over to do." He says he loved and cherished his wife, even in those years when he was on the road for months at a time, "but I never really knew what I had until she was gone.

"God has been good to me," he says. "I ain't necessarily always been good to Him. But He's brought me through a lot of bad times. God never takes His hand off of you. When I lost Mary Agnes, I have to say it made me stronger spiritually. I don't know why. Going through that grief just made me need God more. We're all prone not to call on Him until we need Him pretty bad. And then there's age. Age does a marvelous thing for people. I've often said that God never made a mistake, but if He ever did, it was not giving us our brains back when we were twenty-five or thirty. I worked hard and I've been blessed, and I thank God I'll have a little something to leave my grandchildren. But I've said

The fact is that J. D. always loved the competition, the friendly rivalries. The basses did try to outdo one another onstage, and J. D. always believed he could hit the super-low notes. That confidence made it happen. Was he always the best blender, the smoothest voice? No. He didn't claim to be. But he was always there, doing his best for the total sound and providing that slide to the bottom of the scale at the end of many numbers.

He was a clown, a cutup, always good for a laugh. He also had a reputation for being a pretty rough char-

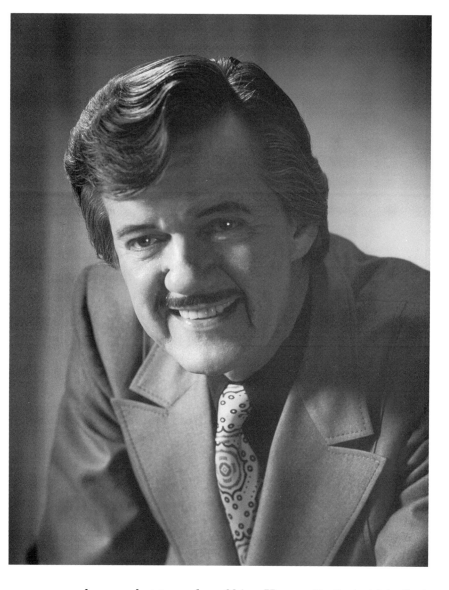

many times, if I could leave my grandson what I know instead of what I've got, he'd be a rich man."

J. D. is the type of performer who makes you remember when you first saw him. Maybe you date that back to when he was a teenager in Florida and the lanky, skinny kid with the prominent nose and ears, and short, wavy hair ambled out and sang with the Sunny South Quartet and later with the Sunshine Boys.

J. D.'s biggest move came, of course, in 1954 when tragedy struck the Blackwood Brothers and he was hired to replace Bill Lyles. That was the toughest thing he had ever done, replacing a recently killed man who was one of the favorite bass singers of all time. "We weren't the same kinda singers or showmen, and I just had to be myself. I feel like I was accepted pretty quick, all things considered."

J. D. worried that people would not accept him when he replaced Lyles. His tall, soft-spoken predecessor had been a rosy-cheeked, bright-eyed, humble man. Now here came another tall bass singer, but J. D. Sumner could have just as easily played a riverboat gambler or a gunslinger on TV. He had a pencil-thin mustache and a swagger. And he was right; at first people didn't know what to make of him. He recalls that at his first concert with the Blackwoods, people fell just short of holding their noses when he sang.

Finally, after not having been a talker or a funny man onstage up to that point in his career, he stepped to the microphone between songs. "Folks," he said, "I just want you to know that I would never expect to replace Bill Lyles. He had a beautiful voice. James tried real hard to find somebody who could match Bill's singing, and he couldn't do it. So he did the next best thing. He went out and hired the best-looking bass he could find."

That broke the ice, convinced J. D. he could be funny, and gave James the confidence to make use of J. D.'s antics whenever necessary.

One of the funniest lines J. D. ever came up with was at a California concert where the host kept reminding the people to be sure to mark their calendars and "come back January 18, unless Jesus comes, for the Blackwoods, Statesmen, Stamps, and Imperials." Every time he'd remind the crowd about January 18, he'd add, "unless Jesus comes."

Finally, J. D. took the microphone. He said, "Now, ladies and gentlemen, you and I both know that whether Jesus comes or whether He don't come, on January 18 there'll still be enough people left here to fill this building. So regardless whether Jesus comes or whether He don't, Hovie Lister and the Statesmen will be here."

Musicians who were there that night attest that J. D.'s line received the loudest and most sustained laugh they'd ever heard in a concert. Some in the crowd got up and walked around until they could gain control of themselves.

J. D. was operated on in the 1980s to have nodes removed from his larynx. His surgeon told him his vocal chords were "longer by far than any recorded in medical history." J. D. said the doctor "wanted to go in and measure my vocal chords, but he never did. Just like on a piano, the longer the string, the lower the note. So wherever I got those long chords, that's where the low singin' comes from.

"A lot of low bass singers learn to growl. But I've always said that if you can't pronounce a word on those low notes, then you're growling and not singing. One time I was in a hotel room with old London Parris. Now London was a good bass singer, but he was jealous of my range and would try to compete with me. It was just me and him in the room and he says, 'J. D., let's hit a few, just two bass singers hitting a few low ones.' I said, 'London, I don't want to hit no low ones.' But he kept on and I finally said all right. I sang the words, 'I love my Jesus' a-way down there as low as I could go and still be understood. Then he tried. He hit the note, but he didn't sing the words. I said, 'No, no. Say "I love my Jesus" like I did.' He couldn't do it. I said, 'If you can't say "I love my Jesus," you ain't got no business singing bass.'"

J. D. was born in 1924 in Lakeland, Florida, about thirty miles from Tampa. He remembers Frank Stamps coming to the Wimauma Church of God camp meeting just outside of Tampa when J. D. was just four years old. "Mr. Stamps sang 'Stand By Me' in his big, powerful bass voice to about 10,000 people without a microphone. My mother says I told her, 'I'm going to be a singer in a quartet and sing like Mr. Frank Stamps.' I don't remember ever even thinking of doing anything else."

J. D. was raised in a church where there were no age restrictions about who was going to sing in the choir. If you could carry your part, you were in. "I was in the choir by the time I was seven or eight years old. My brother was a bass singer, and I tried to sing like he sang. My voice hadn't changed—in fact, I don't remember it ever changing, though it had to at some point. I

J. D. Sumner and the Stamps (from l): Jim Hill, Donnie Sumner (J. D.'s nephew),
Jimmy Blackwood, J. D., and Tony Brown.

sang in the bass section even at that age, so I figure I probably just sang the bass line an octave higher than it was written. It wasn't long, though, before I was singing the note the way it showed in the music."

J. D. was fourteen years old, he says, "when I received Jesus as my Savior. It happened in church. Back in those days, almost every service you had was a revival. We were supposed to have a two-week revival, but it lasted six or eight weeks. There was so many people saved, they couldn't stop the revival. The evangelist had to call the next town and say he couldn't come yet, because God was working too well here."

J. D. first sang outside his own church with three young women—his sister and two cousins. "I sang on

WLAK when I was eight years old and then started going to singing conventions. In the South they had singing conventions almost every Sunday someplace. I think the biggest thrill I ever got was one Sunday afternoon when I was about sixteen and I walked into Polk County Singing Convention in Lakeland. The guy running the singing gig himself said, 'A great bass singer just walked in: J. D. Sumner. J. D., come on up here in the choir.'

"Of all the things that have ever happened to me, I don't think anything thrilled me as much as that. I felt like I was twenty feet tall when he said that."

Jim Wetherington had been born in Ty Ty, Georgia, and moved to Lakeland, J. D.'s hometown, as a young man. So the Big Chief and J. D. were friendly competitors from the time they were kids up until Chief died in the early 1970s. "I loved that boy," J. D. says, still moved by the memory of his friend. "I never knew a better quartet man than Big Chief. A great bass singer."

J. D.'s first job as a professional quartet singer was with the Sunny South Quartet when Big Chief left with Mosie Lister and Lee Kitchens to start the Melody Masters, and J. D. took his place. "I was seventeen years old—had my eighteenth birthday singing in a professional quartet. I never done anything else."

After almost twelve years with the Blackwoods, J. D. moved to the other side of the business in 1967 and took over the Stamps Quartet, which the Blackwoods owned. He managed them, booked them, and served as quartet master. They were soon one of the busiest and most popular quartets on the circuit.

For years J. D. and the Stamps were identified as the backup group for Elvis Presley until his death in 1978. He has long been proud of that association, believing that Elvis knew what he wanted and recognized talent when he heard it. "He could have had his pick of any singers in the world, and he chose us," J. D. says. "That's something you can never take away."

Something else no one can take away from the J. D. Sumner legacy is his incredible creativity. It was J. D. who came up with the idea of quartets traveling by bus. Before that, professional singing groups traveled in seven-passenger cars. The bus idea sounded ludicrous to the Blackwood Brothers, who kidded him that they would rather use a boat or a train. The first bus was so expensive and upkeep so exorbitant that J. D. was nearly laughed out of the business. Today there's hardly a traveling singing group, Christian or secular, that doesn't use a bus.

J. D. got the idea from his time in the military when he was assigned to take wounded soldiers home. They were transported by train or plane and slept in suspended cots. J. D. first tried using springs and mattresses in the buses, but they bounced too much. When he tried mattresses without springs, he had found the solution.

It was J. D. who concocted the idea of the National Quartet Convention in 1956. He envisioned an old camp meeting with all the groups getting together once a year. It has far outdistanced his wildest dreams.

J. D. was also the first to suggest an individual microphone for each singer rather than just one or two for the whole group. The sound and blend have never been the same.

Because of his problem with equilibrium, he often uses a stool on stage, especially on revolving stages. More and more groups are going to stools.

On top of all that, J. D. became a songwriter and has penned more than 500 gospel songs, mostly at the urging and with the encouragement of James Blackwood. He worked quickly, sometimes writing all the songs for an entire album in one long car trip. He played guitar

J. D. Sumner and the Stamps with Elvis Presley.

only a little and used that to sound out his tunes. His lyrics showed a depth of emotion and feeling that surprised people.

One of his classic songs that has been made popular again recently by Sue Dodge's version of it on our tapes is this one:

I Believe in the Old Time Way

In this modern day of living, my, how things have
*   changed.*
People often get religion, but their heart's not changed.
They go to church, they testify, but what an awful fate,
To find they have no real salvation, but will be too late.

Well, I went down to an old camp meeting,
I prayed through in the old time way.
Oh, it was there at an old time altar,
I was saved by amazing grace.

I confessed my sinful living, I was sorry for my sins.
I opened up my heart to heaven, then my God came in.
Now I'm an heir to a home in heaven.
I believe in the old time way.[1]

Though J. D. may have some regrets about his actions in the past, there is no debate that he has been one of the most innovative creative geniuses in our industry for many years.

In 1981 he helped form the Masters V, hooking up with Rosie Rozell, Jake Hess, James Blackwood, and Hovie Lister. For eight years, those legends were back on the road. The personnel in that group continued to evolve as well, as members decided to finally get off the road and take better care of their health. Eventually, J. D. was the only remaining original member, and he didn't feel right about still presenting the group as the Masters V.

One night in 1988, at the National Quartet Convention, J. D. and his guys were introduced to a warm welcome as the Masters V. He had them turn their backs on the audience, and he said, "Ladies and gentlemen, you welcomed the Masters V. Now would you welcome J. D. Sumner and the Stamps Quartet?" The guys turned around to a roar of approval, and the name change stuck.

J. D. has been most appreciative of Gloria's and my efforts to keep bringing these legendary groups back together for video tapings. "You know," he says, "I worked with James and Jake for decades, and we never told one another 'I love you.' We never hugged one another. The feelin' was always there, but we were too big a men, too tough, to go up and hug a man. Me and my daddy was that way to a certain extent, but not long before he died, well, we was kissing one another and telling each other that we loved each other. These video sessions have really brought the love out. We're not spring chickens anymore. Most of us are in our seventies already. We're getting to that age where we could hear anytime that one of us is gone. That does something to you.

"So, I thank God for these videos. Sometimes we'll just get to crying in there, and it makes me awful humble that I'm included. I sit in awe looking around at those great singers. Never in 5,000 years would I have ever dreamed of being in that company. You work all your life to be something, and when you finally get to where you are, you find out you ain't nothing after all. These old friends, bein' able to hug their necks and tell 'em I love 'em, that's worth it all."

J. D. Sumner and the Stamps (from l): Roger McDuff, Donnie Sumner, Jim Hill, J. D. (seated), Jimmy Blackwood (floor).

The late 1940s Speer Family (from l): (top) Mary Tom, G. T., Brock, (bottom) Mrs. G. T., Ben, Rosa Nell.

Ten
A Love Story

Over the last seventy-five years, a gospel singing group called the Speer Family has walked onstage in many different configurations. Not all of the singers have been Speers, but in a very real sense they've all been family. And when they sang, "family" is what the audience felt. Whatever the personnel, the Speer Family has always communicated a warm spirit, a genuine sincerity, and a simple, direct message that felt like home.

When the Speer siblings—Brock, Rosa Nell, Mary Tom, and Ben—got together not long ago with some of the singers, past and present, and a group of friends who had enjoyed their singing over the years, it was like a family singing around the piano after dinner on a warm summer evening. But then, that's what the Speers have done since they began.

The origin of the Speers can be traced to the earliest days of the Vaughan Music Company when one of the instructors was named Dwight Brock. His daughter Lena often played the pump organ when he taught. And one day one of his students was a young man named G. T. (Tom) Speer, an Alabama farm boy looking to singing as a way out of the fields.

The Speer Family in 1953 (back from l): Ben, Joyce Black, Brock, (front from l) Dad, Mom.

Tom was the oldest of eleven children. Farm life was hard, yet among his earliest memories was his mother gathering the family to sing songs like "Unclouded Day." Although she died when Tom was not yet ten years old, her singing had been deeply engraved in the family life. By the time he was twenty, Tom had given his life to God and felt a definite call to be a gospel singer.

About the time Tom lost his mother, there was born in a log cabin in Alabama, to county music school teach-

The 1920 Speer Quartet: Mom, Dad, Aunt Pearl Claborn, Uncle Logan Claborn.

ers, a baby girl named Lena Brock. Several years later, at an all-day singing convention, Lena noticed a tall, rugged young man in the row behind her. Evidently, he noticed her, too, especially when she began to sing.

It wasn't long before Tom Speer was invited home for dinner with the Brocks. Tom and Lena were married in 1920. Years later Tom would grin and tell people that he met a singer's daughter at a singing convention, was married in a singer's home, and raised a singing family.

These two young people who walked the creek banks and sat by the fireside falling in love, walked hand in hand from then on, loving God, loving each

other, and loving their family of four children. All of these loves were expressed in yet a fourth love, writing and singing music.

Just a year after their first son, Brock, was born, Tom and Lena organized the Speer Quartet with Lena's sister and brother-in-law. Before Lena's brother-in-law returned to his carpentry trade, the Speers became a popular group in the South. Dad sang bass, Mom soprano, and the other couple alto and baritone. A few years later, when the other couple quit the group, Tom and Lena began taking their children, Brock and little Rosa Nell, with them when they sang. The children would join in a few songs and then be put to bed while

The 1960 Speer Family (from l): Mom, Brock, Ben, Ginger Smith Laxson, and Dad.

Mom and Dad finished the concert. Over the years their roles grew, and two more children came along.

The singing-teacher parents taught all four children to read music and sing parts, and the Singing Speer Family, made up of Mom, Dad, two boys, and two girls, began competing in the otherwise male-dominated Southern gospel field.

The kids grew up and came and went with their own military stints, college, marriages, and children, so the personnel in the group constantly changed. But it always revolved around Mom and Dad Speer. When Brock became a bass, Dad moved back to his natural baritone, and the group got better and better.

When I was a kid in the 1940s and the Speers came to the Cadle Tabernacle in Indianapolis, Indiana, I never missed them. "Heaven's Jubilee" was the signature Speer song written by Dad Speer. The group sang it at almost every concert for decades.

Heaven's Jubilee

Some glad morning we shall see Jesus in the air,
Coming after you and me, joy is ours to share;
What rejoicing there will be, when the saints shall rise,
Headed for that jubilee, yonder in the skies.

Seems that now I almost see all the sainted dead,
Rising for that jubilee, that is just ahead;
In the twinkling of an eye, changed with them to be,
All the living saints to fly to that jubilee.

When with all that heav'nly host we begin to sing,
Singing in the Holy Ghost, how the heav'ns will ring;
Millions there will join the song, with them we shall be,
Praising Christ thru ages long, heaven's jubilee.

Oh, what singing, oh, what shouting,
On that happy morning when we all shall rise;
Oh, what glory, hallelujah!
When we meet our blessed Savior in the skies.[1]

The Speers eventually started their own music publishing company, and I'll never forget the day Ben Speer called me. He said, "You know, we've been hearing some of these songs that you've been writing, Bill, and we think some of them are pretty good. The other night I heard the Golden Keys sing 'I've Been to Calvary.' Do you have a publisher for that?"

My heart raced. "No."

"Would you be interested in our company publishing that?"

"How does that work?" I asked.

Ben said, "I'll send you a contract, and we'll get started." So he did, and they put "I've Been to Calvary" on a record and sent me my first sheet music. I couldn't

Ann Downing, singing "Joy In the Camp."

believe it. There was the song I had written in 1960 as a young junior high school teacher.

I've Been to Calvary

I've never traveled far around the world,
I've never seen the many thrills and sights unfurled.
But I have taken the journey of journeys for me,
Up Calvary's mountain, there my Savior to see.

I walked the Calvary road where Jesus trod,
I saw Him hanging there, the Son of God!
With tear-stained eyes I knelt and prayed, "Jesus, hear
  my plea";
Oh, praise the Lord! I'm glad I've been to Calvary.

I've been to Calvary, I can say I've seen the Lord;
I've been to Calvary, through the witness of His Word;
Each day at Calvary, what a thrill of love divine,
Just to know that this Savior is mine![2]

Ben Speer has always been a meticulous musician, something he learned from his father. He simply delights in music done correctly and harmonically. He has served as music director on all the "Homecoming" videos, and I'm here to say I could not have done it without him. It has been a joy to get to know him better personally. He is truly the total package of a good heart and musical genius. Mom and Dad Speer were sticklers for accurate singing and both spent a lot of time teaching in gospel singing schools. Brock recalls, "In 1948 we were singing stuff just much like it was in the songbook. Dad and Mom insisted we sing every note exactly right."

One of Brock's fondest memories is of coming to Christ as a child. "We went to the Methodist church in Double Springs, Alabama. That summer, during what we called our protracted meeting, we worshiped in an old tabernacle that my dad, uncle, and some of the men in the church had built. I came and knelt at the altar, and my dad was on the other side of the altar praying for me. I can still see him in my mind, laughing and crying at the same time over seeing one of his kids down at that altar giving his heart to the Lord.

"I've never gotten away from that, always treasured that memory and that experience. I don't have a lurid, dramatic life story to tell you. I wasn't delivered from drugs, crime, or drinking. But I can testify to the sustaining grace of God who's able to keep you."

The day we celebrated the Speer Family in the studio, one of their unrelated alums, Sue Dodge, choking back tears, paid a tribute to Brock:

I think I speak for all of those who have been a part of the Speers over the years when I say that Brock Speer has been one of the greatest influences in my life. I was just a stupid kid when I went with them, and on the road you see stuff. You see people who don't live what they say, whose marriages are in shambles. But not with Brock Speer. He would spend many nights with us on the bus, just talking. When I was struggling with something, he would read Scripture to me and show me the love of Jesus.

I've been married almost twenty years, and I hope we have what Brock and Faye have at the forty-five-year mark. No matter what time the bus pulled in from the road, Brock would get up, clean up, and put on aftershave so he would be presentable to go home to his bride.

He told me when I was about to marry, "I know it's hard for you to leave the road and all the things this holds for you. But I would never deprive you of what I've experienced in my marriage."

I say thank you for all the others. Jeanne and Bob Johnson, Ann Downing, and all the rest say thank you for setting such an example. When everything around us is so unstable, you remained the same, Brock Speer. You remained a godly man who stood for the things that we sing about. I love you and I thank you.

Faye Speer, Brock's wife, says, "People ask us how we can travel and be together virtually twenty-four

Ben Speer, reuniting in the Fort Worth concert with Sue Chenault Dodge, who sang with the Speers in the 1960s.

hours a day. We've never had a problem that way, because we're best friends. Anything we do, we would just as soon do with each other than with anyone else."

The late gospel songwriter Lee Roy Abernathy had a great influence on Brock Speer's life. For twenty years Brock would ride from Nashville to Atlanta to take singing lessons from Lee Roy. Faye says she was never sure whether Brock really wanted to train his voice or just used this as an excuse to spend time with Lee Roy Abernathy.

An imaginative, innovative writer, ahead of his time, Lee Roy Abernathy was the first Southern gospel composer to write a national hit, "Everybody's Gonna Have a Wonderful Time Up There," which sold over a million copies. You haven't really heard a song sung right until you've heard the Speer Family perform that great song.

Everybody's Gonna Have a Wonderful Time Up There

Listen, everybody, 'cause I'm talking to you.
Jesus is the only one to carry you through.
Better get you ready for I'm telling you why,
Jesus is a-coming from His throne on high.

Many are the weary and the lone and sad,
Gonna wish they hadn't done the things they had,
How're you gonna feel about the things He'll say
On the judgment day?

Listen here, my sister, we're not leaving you out.
You may not be the preacher but you sing and shout.
What's the use to worry if you've been redeemed,
Heaven's even better than a miser dreamed;

Think about the trouble you could save some soul,
Tell them what to do to reach the shining goal,
Surely you can show them how to find the light,
Make the whole thing right.

When the tribulations seem to darken the way,
That's the time to get down on your knees and pray.
Everybody gonna have their troubles too,
Gotta be so careful 'bout the things we do;

Going down the valley, going one by one,
Gonna be rewarded for the things we've done,
When we get to Heaven and the promised land,
Then we'll understand.

Now get your Holy Bible in the back of the book,
The book of Revelation, that's the place you must look;
If you understand it and you can if you try,
Jesus is a-comin' from His throne on high.

Readin' in the Bible all the things that He said,
Said He was a-comin' back to raise the dead,

Are you gonna be among the chosen few,
Will you make it through?

Everybody's gonna have religion in glory,
Everybody's gonna be singing that story,
Everybody's gonna have a wonderful time up there,
Oh, glory hallelujah!

Brother, there's a reckoning a-coming in the morning,
Better get you ready 'cause I'm giving you the warning,
Everybody's gonna have a wonderful time up there.[3]

Tom and Lena Speer, even into old age, were precious to watch onstage. They sang with such joy and love, it was infectious. Occasionally Mom Speer would turn to Dad and they would seem to be singing to one another, reminding each other that they had been entwined on this journey of life for years and wanted it no other way.

In the 1960s, when the Speer Family lost Dad and then Mom Speer within eleven months of each other, Brock says, "We lost the whole heart of the group. Nobody lost more out of a singing group than we did then. We didn't know whether we could carry on without them, we depended on them so much." Choked up, Brock adds, "I remember Big Chief Wetherington of the Statesmen said, 'You gotta sing, boy. We're gonna hold you up. We're not gonna let you down. You gonna sing and you gonna make it. We need the good groups. Keep goin'.' That was great encouragement to me."

At Mom Speer's funeral, Dr. Ted Martin spoke of her:

It would truly be like gilding a lily for me to try to eulogize Mom Speer. The many beautiful flowers speak of the love of friends. Your presence here today, and the sweet and beautiful breath of heaven that has swept across our hearts during the singing of these numbers are evidence enough that she was loved on earth and is loved in heaven.

She and her husband pioneered gospel singing because they loved God. Because they founded a ministry, they founded an exciting and meaningful way to make that love known. What greater way to tell the story of salvation, what greater way to let people know what it is to be saved, what it is to be sanctified, what it is to be filled with the Holy Spirit than to sing it until the spirit and the message and the joy and the rhythm of that singing captured the hearts and the lives of the people who heard it.

They sang because they loved each other. You who have heard and seen them sing know the smile of heaven that was on their faces and the tears that stained their cheeks. But you saw, too, those little glances at each other. And you knew not only how they deeply loved God, but also how deeply they loved each other until human love had been given a song, and a song that could carry the message of salvation.

You can't stop that kind of love. It may be that for a little while some that share in that song have their voices silenced here. But they sing on, and the sound of their singing rings within the hearts of those who bear their name, who have their personality, their life, their purpose, and thank God, their Savior and Lord so deeply within their hearts and lives that they sing on. We heard her after Pop's death singing about heaven, and our hearts were touched.

She told someone not long ago, "You know, it won't be too bad to be with Jesus, and with Tom again." This is where she is.

If I could describe what happened in the wee hours of Friday morning I'd tell you of a voice, familiar to her, far more familiar to her than to any of us, who said, in the words of the Song of Solomon, "Rise up my love, my fair one, and come away. For the winter's past, the rain is over, the flowers appear on the earth, the time of singing is come. And the voice of the dove is heard. Arise my love, my fair one, and come away."

Lee Roy Abernathy, one of the first innovators in our industry. A very contemporary writer, he wrote the first million selling national hit, "The Gospel Boogie (Everybody's Gonna Have a Wonderful Time Up There)," made popular by Pat Boone. Lee Roy played with the Homeland Harmony Quartet and the Rangers Quartet, but he also spent a lot of time on his piano playing correspondence course and his songwriting.

Bob and Jeanne Johnson, formerly of the Speer Family

Gloria finished our tribute to the Speer Family with this:

It's a rare thing these days to see a real love story that spans three decades. It's rarer still to see a couple who lived with integrity, who loved their God supremely, and raised their family to love each other and serve the Lord.

Tom Speer's angel, the one he first heard singing alto at the all-day singing convention, is no doubt still singing with him. And their kids, with grandchildren of their own, still sing too. Through the years a long parade of Speer singers has traveled through this group and gone on to their own ministries all over the country. All of us who have sat in their concerts or listened to their recordings have been encouraged, empowered, and enriched by the message and the music.

One day, all the Speers that ever were will gather around the throne of God. Music will reverberate through the golden streets, and should our Lord ask one of the Speers to choose a song, I have a feeling Tom would take his Lena by the hand and sing an old song with a new verb tense. "Heaven IS Worth It All."[4]

Brock Speer, elder member of the Speer Family, singing V. O. Stamps's great "When All God's Singers Get Home,"
from the video of the same name.

(from l) George and Clara Younce with Van and Glen Payne,
partners and friends for more than three decades with the Cathedrals.

Eleven
Fifty Faithful Years

You'd recognize the sound anywhere: the rich, deep bass voice; the clear, resonating lead singer; and the close four-part harmonies. That is the exciting sound that only a Southern gospel quartet can create. Put it all together and you have the Cathedrals, the best-known gospel quartet singing today.

The Cathedrals have been so popular for so long that they have become synonymous with the fan awards presented by *The Singing News*. They have won a slew of Dove Awards and Grammy nominations, but where they really dominate is with their fans. For the last three years running, their supporters voted them the favorite group of the year, Glen Payne as favorite lead, George Younce as favorite bass, Scott Fowler as favorite baritone, Ernie Haase as favorite tenor, and Roger Bennett as favorite instrumentalist. That's an unprecedented sweep that may never be matched.

The sound of the group has always revolved around the two creators of the group, Glen Payne (lead) and George Younce (bass). Over the years several different combinations of great talent have sung the other parts, but the voices of George and Glen have been constant, the reason for their unique sound.

The Cathedral Quartet today (from l): Glen Payne, Scott Fowler, Roger Bennett, George Younce, Ernie Haase.

The 1963 Cathedral Trio (from l): Glen Payne, Danny Koker, Bobby Clark.

"Faithful" is the word that best characterizes these two men. For fifty years now they have given their lives to singing the Gospel.

First, they've been faithful to their Lord. They could have sung about many things, but instead chose to sing of their Redeemer.

They've been faithful to their families, and their families evidence that faithfulness.

They've been faithful to their art form and continue to perfect their performance and communication skills today.

They've been faithful to the beautiful people who have enjoyed their concerts and recordings down through the years.

I've known George and Glen for forty of those fifty years, and "faithful" is, indeed, the best word to describe their friendship as well. I have many friends and loved ones in this business, but none are closer to me than Glen and George. They have been and continue to be the best encouragers in the gospel music field today.

The Stamps-Ozark Quartet, 1955, (clockwise from top): Glen Payne, Fred Bennett, Henry Slaughter, Pat Garner.

In a day when we desperately need role models who have lived out their faith through the good and bad times, I thank God for men like George and Glen.

If George and Glen look familiar, you might notice a resemblance between them and some past TV stars. George is a slightly older and rounder version of Jim Nabors. Glen is a slightly younger version of Art Carney.

Over the years, they've often stopped by our house for breakfast or coffee and gathered around our piano to sing a new song they just learned. When the Cathe-drals are around, it isn't long before you're laughing and having a lot of fun.

Glen recalls that in January 1944 he began his tenure with the late Frank Stamps and the Stamps Quartet with a 6:30 A.M. broadcast. "I was seventeen years old, and to be able to sing that signature quartet song, 'Give the World a Smile,' was a privilege. I knew both writers of that song."

George is just three years younger than Glen, but for years he has made an entire stage bit out of kidding

The 1963 Weatherford Quartet (from l): Bobby Clark, Glen Payne, Danny Koker, Armond Morales, Earl Weatherford.

The 1957 Weatherford Quartet (top l to r): Henry Slaughter, Lily Weatherford; (middle)
Earl Weatherford; (bottom) Armond Morales, Glen Payne.

Glen about his age. When I mentioned that we had a picture of Glen with the Stamps Quartet in 1944, George said, "You mean they took pictures back then? I just love old people."

Glen Payne is one of the outstanding lead singers of all time. A native Texan, he was born in Roy City, just outside of Rockwall, in 1926. When he was eleven years old, his granddad took him to see V. O. Stamps and his quartet at a high school auditorium in Josephine, Texas. Glen remembers that admission cost his granddad a quarter and Glen fifteen cents. It turned out to be one of those unforgettable moments in a kid's life where he just knew nothing would ever be the same again. Glen discovered what he wanted to do with the rest of his life.

By the time he was seventeen, Glen was singing with the Stamps-Baxter Quartet. He had also attended several of their singing schools and became proficient in shaped notes. In 1994, on the fiftieth anniversary of Glen's start in the business, he called the surviving members of the Stamps-Baxter Quartet—all but one are still alive—and asked if they remembered what they were doing that day fifty years before. He reminisced with Jack Taylor,

The Blue Ridge Quartet, 1957, (left): George Younce, Elmo Fagg (top), Bill Crowe, Kenny Gates, and Ed Sprouse.

whom Glen says was "one of the most underrated piano players I've ever heard in all my fifty years—and he can still play this style as good as anybody I ever heard."

Glen also called up Loy Hooker, the original first tenor with the Stamps Quartet, and asked him, "Do you remember what you did fifty years ago today?"

George Younce's first group, the Spiritualaires in the 1940s (from l): Stanley Wilson, Herb Miller, Ike Miller, George, and Willis Abernathy (pianist).

Loy said, "I sure do. I picked you up at 5:30 A.M. in a 1942 Buick."

Glen served in the U.S. Army during World War II, after which he joined the Lester Stamps Quartet. He spent two years with the Stamps All Stars and then went to sing lead for the Stamps-Ozark Quartet in Wichita Falls, Texas. He stayed there six years before being invited to sing lead for the Weatherfords in their ministry at Rex Humbard's Cathedral of Tomorrow in Akron, Ohio. It was there Glen met his love for life, Van Harris, who became his wife on November 30, 1958.

When the Weatherfords moved to Oklahoma in 1963, Glen stayed with the Cathedral of Tomorrow and formed a group called the Cathedral Trio. Glen was the mainstay

The 1964 Cathedral Quartet (from l): George Younce, (seated) Bobby Clark, Glen Payne, Danny Koker.

of the trio's sound. When Rex Humbard suggested adding a bass singer and making the trio a quartet, he recruited George Younce.

George had grown up a fan of the Blue Ridge Quartet, racing home from his job in a furniture factory to turn on their daily afternoon show when he was sixteen. He studied shaped-note singing at a Stamps-Baxter school and sang lead for a local group. Then his voice changed, seemingly overnight, and he has been a bass ever since.

After military service as a paratrooper, George sang with a group called the Watchmen, then sang for the Weatherfords in Akron for a year (the year before Glen joined them) before moving on to the Blue Ridge Quartet. He could hardly believe he was singing with the group he had idolized as a teenager. He sang with them for five years before getting another call from Akron in 1964, one that would set the course for his life. Though both George and Glen had sung with the Weatherfords, they had never met.

They became instant friends as well as coworkers, and when they decided to move the quartet into an independent entity in 1969, they became business partners. And almost starved to death. It took awhile, but with their wives helping run the business, the Cathedral Quartet finally started earning enough money for them to raise their families. Van Payne became secretary to the quartet and still serves in that role. Glen and Van's biggest joy and delight, however, is their family.

The gospel music field is like a big family, and anyone who has Glen Payne as a friend is fortunate. Loyalty to his friends may be his best quality. To spend fifty

The 1980 Cathedral Quartet (from l): Roger Bennett, Mark Trammell, Glen Payne, (seated) George Younce, Kirk Talley.

years in any field and maintain the level of integrity Glen has maintained is almost unheard of. Glen has done it with real dignity and class.

The amazing thing about Glen physically is that his voice has seemed to lose nothing over the years. Now past his seventieth birthday, he still has power and clarity. And whenever I talk about that handful of singers who hit the note right in the middle of the pitch, I always include Glen Payne, even today, more than half a century after he began. He may not have every note in the range he had as a young man, and I would guess he tries to stay away from stringing together too many consecutive songs that tax his lungs. But most of the time you wouldn't guess that the lead singer for the Cathedrals was older than about thirty-five. He's still at the top of his game.

George Younce is pushing the seven-decade mark himself, and he's as dynamic and exciting and powerful a bass as there is on the scene today. That hasn't always been the case with George, however, as he suffered a setback in 1987 that almost took his life.

The Cathedrals were in Englewood, Colorado, when George felt discomfort in the night and was having trouble breathing by morning. He'd had a coronary and was diagnosed with an enlarged and damaged heart. Particularly tough on his family of five children was that he was so far from his home in Stow, Ohio, and they couldn't get to him. His daughter recalls that "when he finally stepped off that plane ten days later, I'll never forget it. It made me realize that family is what's most important. I just thank God every time I see him onstage."

For months, as George recuperated, he was unable to sing a note. His family heard him struggling to try to sing in the shower, and their hearts were broken as he seemed unable to get enough breath to sustain a note. Gradually, his voice returned, but he wondered if he would ever have the old power.

His first concert after his heart attack was in Stuart, Florida. Alone on the bus, he got on his knees and "told the Lord I would sing for Him if He would touch me, because I know that was the only way I could do it."

George had planned to save any taxing bass song until he had warmed up with four or five other tunes, but when he began the program he felt led to start with "The Plan of Salvation." That challenging song features the bass on the verses. "It was far from the best I've ever done, but I knew when I finished that God wasn't through with me yet."

By being careful and maintaining his health over the decade since, George has seen his power and energy return full force. "I probably should have retired long ago," he says, "but I can't imagine that now."

In a day when the whole country is concerned about the family, no family models values more beautifully than the one that George and his wife, Clara, have created. It's encouraging to see kids who truly love and honor their father and mother. George's son-in-law Robbie tells of the first time he saw the Cathedrals:

When I was growing up in Charleston, South Carolina, our youth minister used to take us kids to gospel concerts. I remember the Cathedrals coming to the Charleston Auditorium, and I had never heard of them until that night. Seeing George and Glen and them up there singing changed my life forever. It was just the neatest thing I ever heard in my life.

George remembers that same kid, several years later, coming onto the Cathedrals' bus in the middle of the night and waking him up. "He was nervous," George recalls. "He said, 'G-G-George, c-can I marry Dana?'"

Robbie says, "He told me, 'It's all right with me, son, but Clara's gonna kill ya.'"

The Cathedrals are a group I love for several reasons. First, of course, are Glen and George. They're just great people, wonderful Christians, top musicians, and dear friends. Then they seem to have fun onstage. They know people love to hear them, the harmonies, the crooning, the low notes. And they deliver. They give the praise to God and they entertain and minister to the people.

They're throwbacks to the good old days when groups relied on great piano and innovative songs and arrangements. You can tell this is a group that rehearses long and hard. There's no resting on laurels here. These guys are good and seem determined to stay that way. This is a quartet that was there when the Blackwoods and Statesmen were in their heyday, and they remind us of what quartet singing has been since the 1940s.

It'll be a sad day when Glen and George finally have to hang it up, but they are so encouraging to their young counterparts that it gives us hope that some will keep carrying the torch. There's a lot to be said for contemporary Christian music and all the new styles. But I'm hoping there'll always be a Cathedrals quartet type of a group around. We'll all feel younger that way.

The Cathedrals (from l): Ernie Haase, Scott Fowler, Glen Payne, George Younce, and Roger Bennett.

All day singing and dinner on the ground at Hovie Lister's church, Mount Zion Missionary Baptist Church on Powder Springs Road, near Marietta, Georgia, 1950.

Twelve
A Labor of Love

It's hard to believe there once was a time when life was simple and neighbors could trust each other—when a handshake was more binding than any contract. Would you believe there was a time when learning was a treasured privilege? When children honored their parents and respected their teachers? When parents considered their children God's greatest gift?

Would you believe there was a time when people went to church to stay all day and were never in a hurry to leave? A time when families met to sing together and pray for one another and then spread out a meal to eat together? When no one went home empty in body or in spirit, because there was always plenty of laughter, music, fellowship, and food to go around?

There was such a time, and that's what lovers of Southern gospel music still celebrate. When Gloria and I get together with our old and new friends, we rejoice in the ties that bind: trust, love, honesty, and commitment. There is always much singing and laughing, and yes, crying. I am as moved as any and often find tears rolling down my face.

Something about this music and the history it reminds us of results in stories told, testimonies to the faithfulness of God shared, and strong old friendships renewed. Singing about God and Jesus and salvation and heaven, and directing these praises to the One who makes it all possible even makes us think differently about each other. Our bonds have been mellowed by time and experience. When I sing with old friends, there's always lots of confirming of a truth that perhaps only our histories can teach us: we really do need each other.

You don't need to be a professional or produce a video to enjoy the same heartwarming thrill. Gather around a piano or a guitar, pull out an old songbook, and pick out a part. It may be fun and dramatic when the best of the best gather around and do this, but the beauty of this music and these truths and our God is that they and He are accessible to everyone. Anyone can love and enjoy gospel music.

Having the privilege of immersing myself again in Southern gospel has been a thrill. I was in a unique position—a fan of these people and not really a competitor—to be able to get them together and see what happened. It's been so gratifying to hear from so many of them that the renewed exposure has resulted in new interest in their ministries. Many of them are busier than ever.

What makes this so much fun for me is that I am, at heart, a choir director. And when I have a hundred or more of the greatest legends of gospel singing in a studio or on a stage and I'm digging songs out of the historical catalog of great American tunes, I have the best

Karen Peck, formerly with the Nelons, now has her own group, New River.

choir and the best music in the world. If I look as if I've already gone to glory in some of these cuts, it's because that's how I feel. The music is being interpreted by people who know what they're doing and who are living what they're singing. It's coming from the gut, and they still have the talent to make it sound great. To me, paradise would be an unending videotape and an unending session with singers who never grow tired or hungry.

To get that great sound, everybody has to be doing their part correctly. That's the challenge and that's the fun, and when you have legends in every section, you can't beat it. That's the joy of it for me, and I'm very much at home working on that sound.

When people get together to sing about the Lord and celebrate what He's done in their lives, it isn't long before they find themselves singing about the fact that the Creator of the universe chose to get involved in our daily lives, to actually come to where we are. Sooner or later, someone is bound to be singing about the incredible love of God.

Many writers have written about this incredible love, but none more effectively than V. B. (Vep) Ellis.

The Love of God

The love of God has been extended to a fallen race;
Through Christ, the Savior of all men,
There's hope in saving grace.

It goes beneath the deepest stain that sin could ever
*   leave;*
Redeeming souls to live again,
Who will on Christ believe.

The flowers blooming in the spring, the heavens up
*   above*
In silent declaration
Bring the story of God's love.

The love of God is greater far than gold or wealth
*   afford.*
It reaches past the highest star and covers all the world.
Its power is eternal, its glory is supernal,
When all this earth shall pass away, there'll always
*   be the love of God.*[1]

Part of the heritage we want to pass on to the next generation are the great songs of writers like Cleavant Derricks, an African-American writer whose works have impacted believers everywhere. He's the one who wrote the wonderful, fun song of praise "Just a Little Talk with Jesus."

Buddy Mullins of Mullins and Company was formerly
with the Gaither Vocal Band.

Just a Little Talk with Jesus

I once was lost in sin but Jesus took me in,
And then a little light from heaven filled my soul;
It bathed my heart in love and wrote my name above,
And just a little talk with Jesus made me whole.

Sometimes my path seems drear without a ray of cheer,
And then a cloud of doubt may hide the light of day;
The mists of sins may rise and hide the starry skies,
But just a little talk with Jesus clears the way.

I may have doubts and fears, my eyes be filled with tears,
But Jesus is a friend who watches day and night;
I go to Him in prayer, He knows my every care,
And just a little talk with Jesus makes it right.

Now let us have a little talk with Jesus,
Let us tell Him all about our troubles,
He will hear our faintest cry
And He will answer by and by;
Now when you feel a little prayer wheel turning,
And you know a little fire is burning,
You will find a little talk with Jesus makes it right.[2]

Calvin Newton as an 11-year-old
preacher boy.

When family gets together—and that's what we feel like, old-timers, newcomers, young and old—there's sometimes forgiving and welcoming back business to take care of. One of our guests for the "All Day Singing" video was Calvin Newton, still looking youthful at sixty-five. He shared his testimony of youthful promise, then disappointment, sin, crime, prison, and finally restoration.

Calvin had been a boy soprano who learned to defend himself against teasing by learning to box. When he got into gospel quartet singing, he played the tough-guy role and felt he alienated a lot of his friends. When he used pep pills to stay awake and then got hooked,

Calvin today, after many hard miles and lots of grace.

music. Thirty years later he watched our first "Homecoming" videos with mixed reactions. Many old friends were included, and the love was flowing freely. He felt terrible to have missed so many years.

Finally he wrote me a letter, pouring his heart out and telling me how desolate he felt at having had no outlet for his singing for so long. I told him to get himself to Alexandria for the next taping and to prepare to be loved.

His testimony was one of the high points of that next video, and he was embraced, loved, forgiven, and welcomed back. And now, in his late sixties, he's busier than ever, singing for his Lord.

One of the most moving stories I heard in the tapings was from Donnie Sumner, J. D.'s nephew, for a video called "Joy in the Camp," released in the spring of 1997. Donnie told us that during the Vegas and Elvis years, he got into drugs and really got on the wrong path. He left gospel music, got into secular music, and became a drug addict before eventually coming back to the Lord.

There have been dozens of emotional moments in these videos, but I would have to say this was the most moving I experienced. I've rarely seen a man so contrite and broken. He said simply that he didn't deserve to be there, "but thank God I belong because of the blood of Christ."

People often ask what it is about these simple, not overly produced videos that makes them work on so many levels. From my perspective, their very simplicity is at the heart of it. We get people together who love God and each other and who have wonderful memories of

the friends he had alienated left him. Eventually, despite experience singing with the Melody Masters, the Blackwood Brothers, the Oak Ridge Boys, and the Sons of Song, Calvin found himself sentenced to prison.

There he turned back to Christ, but upon his release did not find himself welcomed back into Christian

The Happy Goodman Family (from l): Vestal Goodman, Howard Goodman, and Johnny Minick.

ministry and victory in Christ, and we just let them sing and talk. Then we stand back and see what God does.

I want to finish with a couple who have been as visible as anyone in the videos, Howard and Vestal Goodman. People are curious about this big-voiced couple with the smiling faces, lined with evidence of their years at the forefront of gospel music.

Many of us who were around in the 1960s remember getting ready for church to the sounds of the "Gospel Singing Jubilee" on Sunday morning television. Our kids looked for their socks and ate their oatmeal, we put on our suits and fed the dog, while the Happy Goodman Family reminded us why we went to all that trouble to go to church instead of sleeping in. It was, they sang, to get in touch with heaven, if only for a few moments, so that we could live all week reminded that this is a journey, and we're not home yet.

When Vestal sings, it's as if you're hearing the message for the first time. It doesn't matter if it's an old hymn or a contemporary song, you just can't help getting into it when she sings. One of the things that has made the Goodmans so infectious is the fun that they have together. It's obvious they believe in and love what they're singing, and have a good time singing it together.

As I've said before, Vestal is one of those singers who hits the pitch right in the middle. Regardless what you think of her range and style and volume, no one can say she isn't perfectly on key. Howard Goodman, who started singing with his sisters and brothers, is a real character who loves to have a good time, tell a great story, and enjoy a good laugh. Men and women like him and Vestal seem to consider each day a bonus—each sunrise, the laughter of a child, the embrace of a loved one, the joy of sights and sounds, all bonuses.

People who live focused on the wonder of life, the goodness of God, and a destination beyond know that death will be only another sunset and that we will all meet again in the morning inside the eastern gate of the city.

Howard says that when he met Vestal she had a high, soft, soprano voice. "We were in a tent meeting," he says, "and so help me, this is what happened. Hurricane Audrey was a fierce one that killed a lot of people in Louisiana, and our tent was right in the path. It leveled our tent to pieces. Everything we had was destroyed. Vestal was sitting there crying, and songwriter Joel Hemphill's dad came by and said, 'Daughter, don't worry. God's got it all under control.'

"That night we were to sing in a church that didn't have a sound system. I sat down at the piano and Vestal handed me an old songbook and said, 'Look at this.' I

The Happy Goodman Family (from l): Sam, Vestal, Howard, Rusty.

*The Happy Goodman Family, 1962, (from l) Rusty, Vestal, Howard, and Sam
with the Life Temple Choir in Madisonville, Kentucky.*

had never played it, but she began to sing the old song 'When Burdens Seem Too Hard to Bear.' And her voice just kept getting bigger and stronger as she sang. God changed her voice that night."

Vestal adds, "I've never been able to sing soft since."

The toughest time on the road for Vestal came when the Goodmans were in Finley, Ohio, at a revival and her daughter Vicki, then about five years old, had been out in the snow at home and had fallen and broken her wrist. "They called me and said, 'Vestal, you need to come home,' but I couldn't get out of the city because of the snow. I cried and I cried. I finally got Vicki on the phone and told her how bad I wanted to be there and that I would pray for her. Then I told the Lord that if he'd just take care of my children, I would sing for Him as long as I lived. And He has done that."

Howard's deepest valley was when Vestal had open-heart surgery in 1974. Mary Tom Speer, their dear friend, went to the hospital and sat with Howard, holding his hand while Vestal was in surgery for seven hours. Howard says, "When they came out and said Vestal was gonna be all right, Mary Tom smiled and left.

Conrad Cook, writer of "Take Your Shoes Off, Moses, You're On Holy Ground."

What a comfort she was and a friend to us both."

So how is it that transient pilgrims with no lasting home can come to be known as the Happy Goodmans, happy, contented, and secure? They will tell you it is the confidence, the blessed assurance, in knowing that Jesus walks the road with them. That's what makes pilgrims joyful on the journey and confident that the destination is worth any struggle.

Howard and Vestal still journey together and show us all why, as they like to say, "defeat" is one word they're not going to use.

From Father Abraham to John the Revelator, from the first-century church to this moment, the people of God have always seen themselves as pilgrims, never settlers. "This world is not my home, I'm just a-passing through" is more than a line from an old song. It's the truth.

The sojourner's theme has been told to children in stories, sent in letters of encouragement to friends, preached from pulpits, and whispered behind closed doors of the underground church in times of persecution. But mostly, it's been sung.

When kings were unjust, subjects sang of a kingdom whose builder and ruler was God. When the world

Nancy Harmon singing her own great song, "The Church of the Living God."

Anthony Burger, former keyboard artist with the
Kingsmen, is now a solo wizard.

We'll Soon Be Done with Troubles and Trials

*Some of these days I'm going home where no
    sorrows ever come,
We'll soon be done with troubles and trials;
Safe from heartache, pain, and care, we shall all that
    glory share,
And I'm gonna sit down beside my Jesus,
Lord, I'm gonna sit down and rest a little while.*

*Kindred and friends now wait for me, soon their
    faces I shall see,
We'll soon be done with troubles and trials;
'Tis a home of life so fair and we'll all be gathered
    there,
And I'm gonna sit down beside my Jesus,
Lord, I'm gonna sit down and rest a little while.*

*I shall behold His blessed face, I shall feel His
    matchless grace
We'll soon be done with troubles and trials;
O what peace and joy sublime in that home of love
    divine
And I'm gonna sit down beside my Jesus,
Lord, I'm gonna sit down and rest a little while.*

*We'll soon be done with troubles and trials,
In that home on the other side,
And I'm a-gonna shake glad hands with the elders
Lord, and tell my kindred good morning,
Then I'm gonna sit down beside my Jesus
Lord, I'm gonna sit down and rest a little while.*[3]

seemed like a foreign country and when the strange language of power and materialism was the accepted tongue, these pilgrims reminded each other that they were natives of a far better place, a place to which they were traveling.

When they were separated, estranged, or lonely, they sang of a great homecoming when all the singers would one day be together around their Father's throne.

During the autumn of our years, Gloria and I look forward to that day when all God's singers get home. That will be the grandest homecoming reunion of them all.

George Younce singing to Claude and Connie Hopper of the well-known Hoppers.

My official sixtieth birthday shot.

There'll be no makeup room, no microphones, no cameras, no buses, no hotel or meal arrangements. We'll be gathered around the throne, smiling, singing, and praising the One we have served in this life.

That is our goal, when our faith shall be sight, and all of God's singers get home. Maybe Gloria said it best when she said, "I like to think that before time began, before the world was created or galaxies were flung into space, there was God—and He was singing a song. The music was so beautiful that it had to be heard. So God created . . . and down through the ages He's always had His singers who picked up the fragments of the melody, hummed bits of harmony, wrote phrases of poetry, or danced short movements.

"No one has ever heard the whole song since that day God sang it alone. But one of these days He will gather all His children home, and one by one the singers of all the ages will lift their voices and fill in the parts that life taught them. At last we'll hear love's sweetest song as it was first conceived in the heart of the great songwriter Himself. It will be perfect. What music there will be when the song of the ages is sung around the Father's throne, when all of God's singers get home!"

With the love of my life, Gloria.

Notes

Chapter One: Homecoming

1. Words and music by James B. Coats. Copyright 1940 by Stamps-Baxter Music. All rights reserved. Used by permission of Benson Music Group, Inc.

2. Words and music by Jim Hill. Copyright 1955. Renewed 1983 by Ben Speer Music. All rights reserved. Used by permission of Integrated Copyright Group, Inc.

3. Words and music by Dottie Rambo. Copyright 1969 by John T. Benson Publishing Company. All rights reserved. Used by permission of Benson Music Group, Inc.

4. Words and music by C. Albert Tindley. Public domain.

5. Words and music by W. B. Stevens. Public Domain.

6. Words and music by Andraé Crouch. Copyright 1966 by Manna Music. All rights reserved. Used by permission.

7. "There Has To Be a Song" by Bob Benson. Used by permission.

Chapter Two: Reunion

1. Words and music by Dottie Rambo and Jimmie Davis. Copyright 1969 by Jimmie Davis Music Company, Inc. c/o Peer Music, Ltd. Used by permission of CPP/Belwin, Inc. All rights reserved.

2. Words and music by Mylon R. LeFevre. Copyright 1963, renewed 1991 by Lefevre-Sing Publishing. All rights reseved. Used by permission of Integrated Copyright Group, Inc.

3. Words and music by Stuart Hamblen. Copyright 1965 by Hamblen Music Company. All rights reserved. Used by permission.

4. Gloria Gaither. Used by permission.

Chapter Three: Old Friends

1. Words by Gloria Gaither. Music by William J. Gaither and J. D. Miller. Copyright 1993 by Gaither Music Company, Always Alive Music, and Life Gate Music. All rights reserved. Used by permission.

2. Words and music by Doris Akers. Copyright 1958 by Manna Music, Inc. All rights reserved. Used by permission.

3. Words and music by William J. Gaither. Copyright 1963. International copyright secured. All rights reserved. Used by permission.

4. Words by William J. Gaither and Gloria Giather. Music by William J. Gaither. Copyright 1969 by William J. Gaither. All rights reserved. Used by permission.

5. Words by William J. Gaither and Charles Millhuff. Music by William J. Gaither. Copyright 1969 by William J. Gaither. All rights reserved. Used by permission.

6. Words and music by Charles (Rusty) Goodman and Jimmie Davis. Copyright 1964 by Jimmie Davis Music Company, Inc. c/o Peer Music, Ltd. Used by permission of CPP/Belwin, Inc. All rights reserved.

7. Gloria Gaither. Used by permission.

8. Mosie Lister, *Good Ol' Gospel—35 All-Time Favorite Songs by Mosie Lister* (Kansas City, Mo.: Lillenas, 1994). All rights reserved. Used by permission.

9. Words and music by Mosie Lister. Copyright 1956. Renewal 1984 by Lillenas Publishing. All rights reserved. Used by permission of Integrated Copyright Group, Inc.

Chapter Four: A Little History

1. "Give the World a Smile Each Day," Words by Otis Deaton. Music by M. L. Yandell. Public Domain.

Chapter Five: The Pioneers

1. From personal interview with Jerry Jenkins and written material contributed by James Blackwood, Sr. Used by permission.

Chapter Six: Clanton

1. Words and music by Mosie Lister. Copyright 1953 WB Music Corp. All rights reserved. Used by permission.

2. From personal interview with Jerry Jenkins and written material contributed by James Blackwood, Sr. Used by permission.

3. From personal interview with Jerry Jenkins and written material contributed by James Blackwood, Sr. Used by permission.

4. From personal interview with Jerry Jenkins and written material contributed by James Blackwood, Sr. Used by permission.

5. From personal interview with Jerry Jenkins and written material contributed by James Blackwood, Sr. Used by permission.

6. From personal interview with Jerry Jenkins and written material contributed by James Blackwood, Sr. Used by permission.

Chapter Seven: Another Living Legend

1. Words and music by Marvin P. Dalton. Copyright 1948 in "Guiding Hand" by Stamps Quartet Music. Renewed 1976 by Stamps Quartet Music. All rights reserved. Used by permission of Integrated Copyright Group, Inc.

2. Words and music by Mosie Lister. Copyright 1955, renewed 1983 by Lillenas Publishing Co. All rights reserved. Administered by Integrated Copyright Group, Inc., P.O. Box 24129, Nashville, TN 37202. Used by permission.

3. Words by William J. and Gloria Gaither. Music by William J. Gaither. Copyright 1976 by William J. Gaither. All rights reserved. Used by permission.

Chapter Eight: The One and Only

1. "Prayer Is the Key to Heaven (but Faith Unlocks the Door)." Copyright 1955 by Duchess Music Corporation. Copyright renewed. Rights Administered by MCA Music Publishing, a division of MCA, Inc., 1755 Broadway, New York, NY 10019. International copyright secured. All rights reserved.

Chapter Nine: The Innovative Genius

1. Words and music by J. D. Sumner. Copyright 1959, renewed 1987 by Gospel Quartet Music. All rights reserved. Used by permission of Integrated Copyright Group, Inc.

Chapter Ten: A Love Story

1. "Heaven's Jubilee," words by Adger M. Pace, music by G. T. Speer. Copyright 1935, renewed 1967. Assigned to W. E. Winsett Music Co., Ellis J. Crum, Kendallville, IN 46755. All rights reserved. Used by permission.

2. "I've Been to Calvary," words and music by William J. Gaither. Copyright 1960 Ben Speer Music, 54 Music Square West, Nashville, Tennessee. Used by permission.

3. "Everybody's Gonna Have a Wonderful Time Up There," words and music by Lee Roy Abernathy. Copyright 1947 Polygram International Publishing, Inc. All rights reserved. Used by permission.

4. Gloria Gaither. Used by permission.

Chapter Twelve: A Labor of Love

1. "The Love of God," words and music by V. B. (Vep) Ellis. Copyright 1949, renewed 1977 in "Supreme Joy" by Stamps Quartet Music. All rights reserved. Used by permission of Integrated Copyright Group.

2. "Just a Little Talk with Jesus," words and music by Cleavant Derricks. Copyright 1937 by Stamps-Baxter Music. All rights reserved. Used by permission of Benson Music Group, Inc.

3. "We'll Soon Be Done with Troubles and Trials." Words and music by Cleavant Derricks. Copyright 1934 by Stamps-Baxter Music. All rights reserved. Used by permission of Benson Music Group, Inc.

Index

We want to hear from you. Please send your comments about this book
to us in care of the address below. Thank you.

ZondervanPublishingHouse
Grand Rapids, Michigan 49530
http://www.zondervan.com